Cities and Courts In the Milan to Venice

Enrico Massetti

Cities and Courts In the Po Valley
Milan to Venice

Enrico Massetti

Copyright Enrico Massetti 2014

Published by Enrico Massetti

All Rights Reserved

ISBN: 978-1523206315

From Milan to Venice

This itinerary has a distinct character of its own, and converge upon a city which, apart from evolving an extremely original way of life and a unique artistic style of its own, exerted an influence far beyond that of the usual medieval or Renaissance city-state: Venice.

This magical city quite rightly appears twice in our travels: the first time, in an excursion which, dedicated as it is to the Renaissance in the Po Valley, includes the capitals of the ancient principalities, those court centers whose magnificence greatly contributed to the enrichment of European culture: Milan of the Visconti and the Sforzas, Mantua of the Gonzagas, Verona of the Scaligers, Ferrara and Modena of the Earnest; and tiny Sabbioneta, whose present countrified aspect still offers evidence of the brave and passionate dream of its one great prince, Vespasiano Gonzaga.

Among these cities, which might rightly include Bergamo, Brescia, and Vicenza which, though not capitals, nevertheless carried the figurative arts and the art of living to the highest level of expression, Venice occupies a unique position.

The itinerary also passes near two lakes: Iseo Lake and Garda Lake, on their own worth a visit.

The itinerary:

Milan

Via Dante

Taking a stroll around Milan is an excellent way of getting to know some fascinating corners. It also the only way to get acquainted with its flavor and life style. It is true what is told about the Milanese who are always in a hurry. However, even if nobody could deny Milan is a very active city, its citizens have learned when to stop and how to enjoy a walk in the city center pedestrian areas while having an aperitif and a good chat with some good friends.

Castello Sforzesco

The city centre pedestrian areas:

Corso Vittorio Emanuele is a pedestrian precinct with the main cinemas, bookshops, fashion shops and bars with open-air tables.

Piazza San Babila – Start of the pedestrian precinct, a square surrounded by post-war architecture with many fashionable shops.

Via Della Spiga – pedestrian street where the great stylists have their showrooms

Brera is one of the most attractive streets with fine private houses, art galleries, original shops most popular for its bars, clubs, restaurants and night-life.

Loggia dei Mercanti, via Mercanti

Via Mercanti – pedestrian precinct with its attractive *piazzetta*, the administrative and political center of Medieval Milan

Via Dante created in the late 19th century to provide an evocative link between the Duomo (cathedral) and the Castle (Castello Sforzesco)

A recommended itinerary:

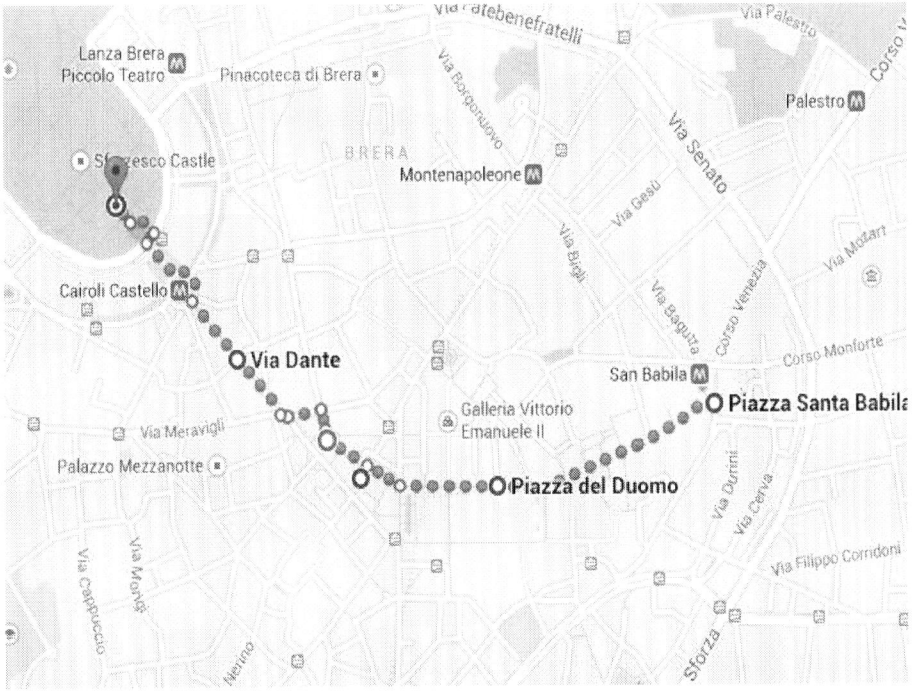

Start from Piazza San Babila, easily reachable with the *metropolitana* underground line 1, station San Babila. You walk in Corso Vittorio Emanuele, a fashionable street with lots of high end shops, mainly clothing.

The roof of the Duomo

A visit to the roof of the Duomo is a **must**. Take the elevator in the back of the Duomo, if you don't want to gasp on an interminable stair!

From the rooftop you are in a magic world of marble and statues, several thousand statues, indeed. Go to the front of the roof and look down at the Duomo square. Look also up to *the Madonnina* the golden statue on top of the highest *guglia*, it's the most loved symbol of Milan.

During World War II it was covered so that it would not shine in the night attracting the attention of the allied bombers.

The Duomo from La Rinascente Cafe

At the end of the Corso you arrive at the back of the Duomo cathedral. Do not miss a visit to the cafeteria of the La Rinascente store under the porticos on your right. You find it by going up to the last floor of the store, the cafeteria has a glass wall facing the top of the Duomo. The sight is unique and the *Cappuccino* is worth a visit too.

Continuing North, you reach the main square Piazza Duomo, in front of **Il Duomo**. You should visit the cathedral of the Duomo, if you have not yet done so.

Galleria Vittorio Emanuele II

On the right you then enter the Galleria Vittorio Emanuele II, the first mall realized in the 19th century, and still a masterwork of artistic shopping.

On the side of the central octagonal don't miss the bull, there is a tradition in Milan: squeezing your feet on the bull's balls is supposed to bring you good luck!

Returning back to piazza Duomo, visit the Piazzetta Reale, on the opposite side of the square: the *Palazzo Reale* is the place where most exhibitions of art are held in Milan.

Continue then towards the right corner of the square, and enter via Mercanti, stopping to look at the Mercanti square on the left: it is a surprising corner of medieval Milan preserved intact to the current days.

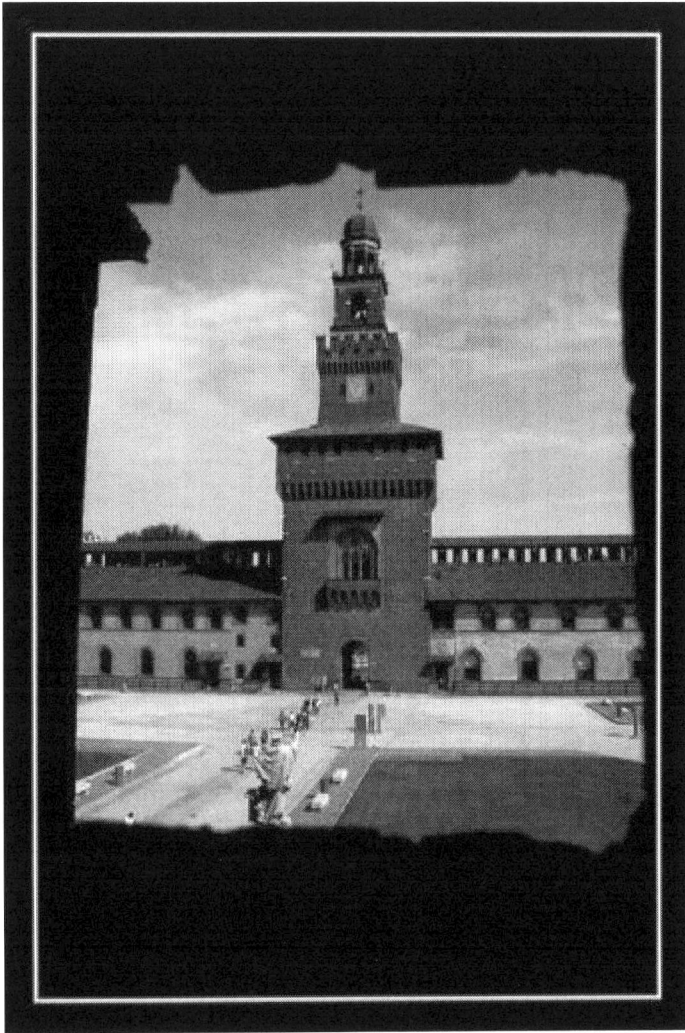

Castello Sforzesco - Milan

At the end of via Mercanti you continue through piazza Cordusio towards via Dante, a pedestrian area. Via Dante will take you to the **Castello Sforzesco**, definitely worth a visit too.

Milan art and shopping

Brera

Today we start from Piazza Scala, easily reached with the underground lines MM1 and MM3 from Piazza Duomo through the Galleria Vittorio Emanuele, or directly with several tram lines, the lines 1 and 2 stop right in the piazza.

The world famous La Scala Theater and its museum can be visited: check on the La Scala web site for schedule and availability of tours: http://www.teatroallascala.org/en/

Piazza Scala with the theater

From Piazza della Scala we take via Giuseppe Verdi, on the right of the Theater, and we make our way to the XVIII century Palazzo Clerici to see the great fresco which Gian Battista Tiepolo palm Led in 1740, entitled, The Course of the Sun, Via Verdi becomes Via Brera, and we come to the Brera, a distinguished building designed by Richini with an austere courtyard, in the center of which stands Canoed's Statue of Napoleon (1809), inspired by classical models. This great gallery contains several masterpieces of Italian art from the XIV to the XX century such as: Raphael's Marriage of the Virgin"; Giovanni Bellini's Pieta'"; Piero della Francesca's Urbino Altarpiece"; Andrea Mantegna's The Dead Christ"; Caravaggio's Supper at Emmaus"; and Bramante's Christ at the Column". There are also six new halls dedicated to Italian paintings between XIII and XVI century; and a collection of metaphysical paintings, in addition to the Maria and Emilio Jesi collection, which has been donated to the gallery.

Brera is an extremely important picture gallery, as is the astonishing collection of paintings left to the city in 1571 by Gian

Giacomo Poldi Pezzoli, which can be reached from the Brera by taking Via Borgonuovo and Via Manzoni. A visit to the two galleries will take up most of the morning.

For lunch go somewhere close by – we recommend Latteria San Marco in Via San Marco, 24, a 7 minutes walk from the end of via Brera, recommended also by Slow Food, a very small place with genuine Milanese cuisine. The place is tiny and doesn't take reservations, so if you want to get one of the 8 very popular tables, arrive when it opens or wait until when a few tables will free up as the early-lunching tourist clientele clears out and the locals take over. After lunch we will continue our tour in the afternoon by wandering through the enchanting streets of romantic Milan, dear to Stendhal.

Via della Spiga

Choose the area delimited by Via Montenapoleone, the modern center of fashionable Milan, Via Sant'Andrea, Via Manzoni and Via delta Spiga. This is the area where you can do the most expensive shopping in Milan, be prepared to spend as much as $6,000 for a skirt, if you want, and can afford it! Fortunately you don't have to buy anything, you can get by with some inexpensive window-shopping. Also go along Via Borgospesso, Via Santo Spirito and Via del Gesu, where you will be struck by the theatrical perspectives of the XVI century Palazzo Bagatti Valsecchi.

Enter the courtyards, where to your astonishment you will discover, among the splashing fountains, the green lawns and the elegant arcades, an atmosphere of quiet you would have never expected to find in the heart of the city.

Villa Reale

Milan, villa Reale

You can then go on to the Public Gardens, or the Royal Villa. This villa is an interesting example of Italian Neo-Classicism: it was designed by Leopoldo Pollack in 1790 for Count Ludovico Barbiano di Belgiojoso, and it was used as a residence by Napoleon before becoming royal property. To the right of the facade facing the street, there is the Padiglione d'Arte Contemporanea (PAC, contemporary art gallery) designed in 1948-54 by Ignazio Gardella. This museum is recommended, you should be sure not to miss it.

Where to eat in Milan:

Restaurants in Milan:

- Nerino Dieci Trattoria Via Nerino 10, +39 02 3983 1019 The service from staff is attentive and they are very generous in their freebies. You are given a complimentary glass of Prosecco on arrival and free bottomless Limoncello after the meal. The quality of food is just spectacular.

- Da Vic - Ristorante Guerrini Via Gaetano Previati, 21, +39 02 4351 5186 If you are looking for a restaurant the locals appreciate, this is one of them. No surprises, no fusion food and good so. You are greeted with a glass of prosecco and then spoiled by excellent choice of Italian food, whether fish, pasta or meat. Superb service, good wine recommendations. Chef personally comes to greet all the clients, which is very appreciated.

- L'Immagine Ristorante Bistrot Via Varesina 61, +39 02 3926 4564 The location and ambiance tell you this is not a place that survives on tourist trade although I am sure many "out of towners" find it via rave reviews. Service is prompt and direct, but a little help with wine and food selection seems to be a welcome custom.

- Da Cenciaioli Via Ferrucci 1, +39 02 495 27 845 Excellent quality and good choice of typical Tuscan products: the lamprey to Morellino di Scansano. Sympathy and veracity heavy enough to ensure the authentic Tuscan. Really excellent meat served well so that it remains hot until the last cut. Service rightly trattoria but adequate prices to the Milan market and product quality.

- Bufalatte via Pavia 3, +39 02 39 81 16 28 Bufalatte offers buffalo mozzarella for take away and some meals including mozzarella, tomatoes, San Daniele ham and some fresh bread. I can recommend Bufalatte to anyone who likes mozzarella and would like to taste the real Deal.

Bergamo Alta - Upper Town

Setting off from Milan down the Autostrada on the morning of the third day of our trip, we reach, after some 30 miles, the city of Bergamo, well worth one day visit.

Bergamo Alta - Piazza Vecchia

Piazza Vecchia – (Old Square)

Piazza Vecchia is the symbol of the city. Built in 1300, it reaches its actual structure during the Venetian domination. On the southern side of the square faces the Palazzo della Ragione, which is the symbol of the Communal Age; on the right side the Civic Tower (XII-XV) rises, well known as Il Campanone, and here there is also the antique Domus Suardorum (XIV-XV), that now is the seat of the University of Bergamo.

The northern side of the square is enclosed within a Palace built in the 1600s with a facade of white marble. Built as seat of the Town Hall, today this structure hosts the Public Library "A. Maj" that holds about 500,000 volumes and preserves a precious "*Tasso Collection.*"

The elegant Fountain, donated by the Venetian *podesta'*, Alvise Contarini (XVIII), completes the spectacular view of the square.

A portico in the Old Town

Behind the Palazzo della Ragione, there is the Piazzetta del Duomo, where there are monuments of great relevance. The Duomo, designed by Filarete, was modified many times during the centuries. The decoration of the interiors was completed only at the end of '800.

Precious artistic pieces are the Chapel of the Crucifix, that preserves a crucifix of '500 and the apse, where seven great canvases, out of all the Martirio di S.Giovanni Episcopo (S. Giovanni Episcopo's Martyrdom), a work of G.B.Tiepolo can be found.

On Piazzetta Duomo, a marble polychrome porch with polychromatic lions by Giovanni da Campione, signals the access to the Basilica di S.Maria Maggiore (XII). Inside, precious tapestries, a baroque confessional by Andrea Fantoni, Gaetano Donizetti and his Master Simone Mayr.

Of great value are the iconostases in carved and inlaid wood executed in the XIV, following Lorenzo Lotto drawings, by G.F. Capoferri and Giovanni Belli. Adjacent to the Basilica is the Cappella Colleoni (XV). Realized on G.B Amadeo project, this Chapel is the mausoleum of the famous condottiere Bartolomeo Colleoni.

Basilica Facade

The polychrome marble facade connects the porch of the Basilica and the rich decoration, while it records the adventurous life of the *condottiero*, it represents a magnificent example of Lombardy Renaissance. Beside the Cappella Colleoni, a flight of steps leads to the access of the Curia Vescovile.

Once one crossed the Aula della Curia, a room with splendid frescoes (XI-XII), there is a courtyard, where, in its center, one finds the Tempietto di S.Croce (S.Croce Temple) built in XI and changed in '500. The last building that decorates Piazzetta Duomo is the Baptistery.

Built in 1340 by G. da Campione as the baptismal basin for the Basilica, it was rebuilt, after various journeys and manipulations, in the place where now it is placed. The interior presents interesting high-reliefs representing the life of Christ. The baptismal source and the S.Giovanni sculpture were realized by G. da Campione.

Basilica di Santa Maria Maggiore

Panoramic view with Basilica di S. Maria Maggiore

Situated in the heart of the upper town, **Basilica di S. Maria Maggiore** is considered the most important monument of the town.

The collocation itself, in the center of the built-up area, underlines the importance of this building. *Piazza Duomo* (Dome Square) has been for a long time, until the building of the close *Piazza Vecchia* (Old Square), the fulcrum of the civil and religious life of the town. The *Duomo*, the *Basilica* and the *Palazzo della Ragione* (the ancient municipality building) face it.

Built in XII, as a vow to the Virgin, the basilica conserved at the outside the original Romanic structure. The ground plan is in the shape of a Greek cross, but the interior, modified in '500 and in '600, is sumptuous.

Many artists worked for its realization: from Lombardy, Venice, Tuscany and foreign artists. There are two entrances to the basilica decorated with precious **porches** of polychrome marbles by Giovanni da Campione (1353-60). The interior is rich of very valuable works.

Wooden Choir Inlays

Wooden Choir inlays

The inlays of the wooden *choir* and the marquetries of the iconostasis represent biblical stories, they were executed between the 1524 and the 1555 on the drawings of Lorenzo Lotto, by the Master G.F. Capoferri and G. Belli: the different chromatic types are due to the different kind of wood, while the color shades and the deepness of the image are obtained with herbs infusions and the use of hot sand.

In the transept there are frescoes of the **fourteen century** by an unknown author from the Lombardy school *(Storie di S.Egidio –* "S.Egidio histories", *l'Ultima cena,* "Last supper", *L'Albero di S.Bonaventura, "Saint* Bonaventura's tree")*. The great Crucifix that hangs on the balustrade of the presbytery is a work by an unknown artist as well. Beautiful Florentine and Flemish tapestries decorate the walls of the basilica. At the end of the nave, there are the monuments of the famous compositor **Gaetano Donizetti** and of his Master **Simone Mayr.** In the left aisle, the precious **baroque** confessional by Andrea Fantoni (1704 – 1705) presents an apology of the confession.

La Cappella Colleoni – Colleoni Chapel

Cappella Colleoni

The *Cappella Colleoni* was built in 1472 when Bartolomeo Colleoni, famous *condottiero* of the *Serenissima* and Captain of the Venetian army, decided to build his own mausoleum. Colleoni ordered it to be demolished by his soldiers due to the sacristy of S.

Maria Maggiore, in spite of the refusal of the canonical people of the basilica.

A cultured and modern man, Colleoni designed a monument that was placed in the heart of the urban space and determined new perspectives (for this reason since 1474 the demolition of the Palazzo della Ragione was established. The project was built by Giovanni Antonio Amadeo, a sculpture-architect that was engaged with the great project of the Certosa di Pavia.

Anyway, the task was very complicated: he had to organize a sacred space that would have preserved the Captain coffin, that would have been apt to the sacred celebrations and that would have found at least a formal harmony with the basilica beside it. Thus, the octagonal tambour of the chapel and the pointed pinnacle of the lantern refer to the fanciful end of the basilica, while the exuberant polychromy of the facade recalls, for the colors and the materials, the portal of the basilica by Giovanni da Campione of the fourteenth-century.

The intellectual interests of Colleoni meet and integrate the availability to the figurative experience by giving life to the Colleoni Chapel: a unique work, made of strictness, transgression, refinements and exhibitionism. (Walter Barbero).

In the interior, the Colleoni monumental grave presents two overlapped sarcophagi inserted in a triumphal arch, a re-elaboration of the monumental gothic graves whose characters, that belong more distinctly to the Renaissance are in any case recognizable in the bas reliefs and in the sculptures, a testimony of the extraordinary plastic capacities of Amadeo. In the second sarcophagus, a *wooden equestrian statue* of Colleoni by Sisto and Siry da Norimberga (1501). In the cupola, in the lunette of the vault, splendid *frescoes of G.B. Tiepolo* (1733) that represent the Virtue and some episodes of the life of S. Giovanni Battista.

On the left wall the *Tomb of Medea*, preferred daughter of Colleoni, work of Amadeo; on the front a high relief, the *Pietá* (1470). Below: a wooden bench containing a biblical inlay by G.Caniana (1785). In the presbytery, the *altar* by B. Manni (1676) by L.Pollsk; in the lunette the *Martirio di S. Bartolomeo* (S .Bartolomeo Martyrdom) by G.B. Tiepolo and *S. Marco Evangelista* by *Tiepolo*. On the walls: the *Sacra Famiglia* (Sacred Family) by *M.A. Kauffmann*; wooden pews with carvings by *G.A Sanz* and *biblical marquetries* by *Caniana* (1773)

Le mura venete – (Venetian Walls)

Rocca di Bergamo

The Upper Town walls, that existed since the Roman Age, documented in VIII, were re-built during the medieval period and they were re-managed and modified more and more times. There are some traces that today are still visible in *via Vagine*, below the convent of *S. Grata* and on the left of the walls avenue, at the west side of the funicular line (ex *via degli Anditi*). At the beginning of the sixteenth century, the walls were in extremely terrible conditions. In 1556, the Venetian Republic, that had been holding the politic and territorial power of Bergamo for more than one century, decided to proceed with the whole reconstruction of the fortification town walls.

The political aim of the Venetians was to enforce the border of their territory of which Bergamo constituted the western extremity and the closest stronghold of the enemies of the Spanish Emperor as well.

Engaged against the Turkish on the opposite front, Venice showed its intention to not expand its power in the Lombardy. The *Serenissima* decided to realize a bastioned stone fortification, since it had abandoned a first project of a partial reconstruction and re-management of the medieval walls, for which also Orologi and Malacrida were consultants and that caused moreover the achievement of the S. Marco Forte and five new bastions in 1561.

Porta San Giacomo

In order to erect the town walls, more than 250 single building were demolished and some areas of the Upper Town were transformed from their natural aspect. The demolitions were necessary to save the building expenses, to shorten the time of realization and, in some cases, for the lack of alternative possible solutions. Thus, many important works and historical monuments got lost, such as the palaeo-Christian Cathedral of S. Alessandro, 80 houses in Borgo Canale, S. Lorenzo churches with 59 houses of the homonym village, S. Giacomo, S. Pietro, S. Stefano with the monastery (transferred in 1571 in the present S. Bartolomeo monastery in the Lower Town), SS. Barnaba and Lorenzino in the neighborhood of S. Giacomo Gate and the sewer dated back to the Roman Age.

In 1574, Bergamo houses were 445; they corresponded to half of the ones that existed before the building of the walls whose perimeter was completed in 1588 under the guidance of the General Sforza Pallavicino. The walls, that constituted one of the most significant fortresses realized by Venice on dry land, were never used for military actions even if the result, as concerns the defensive conception, led the way for that time.

At the beginning of the last century the walls were demilitarized and around them was the inner boulevard, shaded by horse-chestnut trees and plane-trees; the embankments were abolished and the green areas that overlooked the terraces and the bulwark were reduced. Underneath the walls, the agriculture and horticultural activities, that already existed, were consolidated. Also nowadays, they give to the surroundings a beautiful and unique landscape. The walls, that now are partially a communal property and partially public land, were totally rebuilt and in some parts restored in 1976 thanks to the initiative of the *Azienda Autonoma di Soggiorno (Tourist Office)* and for some parts also in 1984. The excursions in the basement and in the embrasure of the walls are possible only upon booking, with the accompaniment of the experts of the speleological group Le Nottole (tel.035 251 233).

The Venetian Walls Gates (XVI)

Venetian Gates

Observing the sections of the gates is easy to determine how they were designed to carry out two main tasks: at the first floor passages and the guardians for the traffic control, the collection of the duties and the urban vigilance; above the openings, towards the outside there were mechanisms for the portcullis and the drawbridge. These gates accomplished a third function: they had to be a symbol of security and proud for the citizens; a source of admiration, respect and reprimand for the foreign people. (G.Della Chiesa).

The usage of building the most decorated facade of the urban gates towards the outside, it is emphasized here by the topographical position and it shows the double function of the walls as well; that means to be an enclosure and a defensive structure but also a balcony, a place for the parades. (V.Zanella)

How to reach the upper town:

From Piazzale Marconi (**Bergamo Stazione**) and from Porta Nuova bus 1 + *funiculare* (Funicolar)

Bus 1 Colle Aperto from the upper funicular station, or enjoy walking in the old city of Bergamo Alta to reach your destination.

Where to eat in Bergamo Alta

Restaurants in Bergamo Alta:

- Ristorante Il Ducale Via Beltrami 12, Citta Alta, Bergamo +39 035 428 4223 Bright, spacious, pretty cool. Menu of fish, all presented well and taste great. Portions sufficient. And 'one of the few places where the shape is synonymous with insight into substance. And in this case, for me, the quantity becomes infinitely negligible.

- Relais San Lorenzo Ristorante Hostaria Piazza Mascheroni, 9, Bergamo +39 035 237383 Modern rooms, classy, clean design with high quality furnishings. Kitchen is wonderful and probably the best in Bergamo old town for just a little more than what you pay for others. Staff highly trained and professional.

- Ristorante Lalimentari Via Tassis, 3a, Bergamo Alta +39 035 233043 A small restaurant just 3 minutes walk from the Piazza Vecchia on a small quiet street. Cozy atmosphere, great food, young cheerful personnel ready to suggest local dishes and wine. You can have a very pleasant time dining and joking with waiters.

- La Tana Via San Lorenzo, 25, Bergamo +39 035 213137 Nice staff, nice ambiance, very good food. In this restaurant they serve traditional recipes with a modern twist. you can have polenta con spezzatino di cervo, tagliata d'oca, verdure grigliate. They are extremely tasty and cooked to perfection. Service is efficient. Make sure you book in advance.

- Colleoni dell'Angelo Restaurant Vecchia 7, Bergamo +39 035 232596 It's nice to sit outside but if the night is hot opt to sit inside. Spacious, not noisy, elegant table settings and attentive service. Food is mostly fish and fairly traditional but very well done. The desserts are especially good. Not a place were you take little kids to, it's more for adults and bigger kids

- <u>Osteria della Birra</u> Piazza Mascheroni 1/c, Bergamo +39 035 24 24 40 Superb selection of brews, Stout and Bitter excellent. The board of Cheese and hams is both excellent quality and value. Great for a drink or a Lunch. Good atmosphere and the staff are very friendly and helpful. The prices are reasonable too.

- <u>Trattoria Parietti</u> Via C. Beltrami 52, Citta Alta, Bergamo +39 035 221072 The tratoria is well worth a visit if you like to eat shoulder-to-shoulder with a room full of Italians having a great time. It is a bit noisy, but very good fun. The portions are huge, so do not order too much!

Iseo Lake

Iseo Lake

We leave Bergamo in the direction of the Iseo Lake, going through Seriate, an old village on the banks of the River Serio, and then Trescore, with important frescoes by Lotto in the Oratory of Villa Guardi. After passing the romantic Lake Eudine, we reach (25 miles) the town of Lovere at the far end of the Lake of Iseo and start off down the eastern shore. Near Pisogne, we find the Sanctuary of S. Maria della Neve with frescoes by Romanino (1540); the road descends amidst magnificent scenery towards the Punta alle Croci Bergamasche and runs along beside the lake: from Sulzano you can take a boat to the Island of Mont'Isola (the largest in any of the Italian lakes) which fills the middle of the lake with its conical mass.

Where to eat in Lovere:

Restaurants in Lovere:

- Bar Centrale Via Gregorini 2, +39 035 960 448 This place is right on lago d'iseo with spectacular views. Very large menu. Food is delicious and the ice cream deserts are incredible!! Save room for them!

- Parol Osteria Vicolo Caserma 4, +39 035 960 818 Although the restaurant is situated in an alley, without sea view, you should go! Service and politeness are a 10 out of 10 Food is fabulous And they have a changing table for baby's in the lady's room. We definitely come back again

- La Lanterna Via Matteotti, 6, +39 035 983 384 If you only visit one pizzeria in Lovere, make sure it's La Lanterna. A fantastic selection of beers and amazing pizzas can be found in this cavernous bar. The bar staff are friendly and incredibly accommodating - they were happy to put the rugby on for us (even if they weren't sure what it was!)

- Fi Che Foi Via Gramsci 2, +39 035 983 380 A genuine rustic wine bar, yet very modern in its atmosphere! Good knowledge about the wines of the area combined with a service minded sense of the staff/owners. Go there for the wines and as far as the food goes you can have some snacks of cheese and ham, which is brilliant.

- La Campagnola via Giorgio Paglia, 48, +39 035 962 005 Friendly atmosphere and very pleasant outside dining area. Good value. Seafood spaghetti good and chef very accommodating.

- Ristorente Mas Via Gregorini, 21, +39 035 983 705 The food's the thing here. It is a small and unprepossessing place. At the back it is almost like an informal family dining area, the front stark and modern. Compared to other restaurants in the town the price is just a little over the average but not much and still very reasonable.

Franciacorta

Franciacorta

Franciacorta, just south of the Iseo Lake, is well worth a visit for its wines; however it offers the connoisseur more than just its famous little bubbles.

Row upon row of vines, gently rolling hills, charming villages, castles and abbeys, battlemented towers, and patrician villas immersed in ancient and verdant landscape is covered by the Strada del Vino Franciacorta. Its evocative landscape is rich in important artistic heritage. This wine region has always been an important centre for commerce, as proved by its many markets, trade fairs and exhibitions held throughout the year. Just a few examples are the annual Carnival at Erbusco where the "Re del Gnoc" is elected and the "Settimana della tinca al forno" (oven baked tench), the fair held in Clusane d'Iseo every summer. The Autumn months are awash with wine tasting events; The "Consorzio per la Tutela del Franciacorta" holds a weekend wine tasting event every September giving participants a chance to find out more about the wines of Franciacorta and the land. The Strada del Franciacorta organizes La Caccia al Tesoro, a Treasure Hunt that leaves no stone unturned; it's an occasion in which to learn about the history, culture and wines of Franciacorta. One of Franciacorta's most longstanding fairs the "Fiera del manzo pasquale" held in Rovato, and now known as Lombardia Carne, was first held on 15 April 1868 under the auspices of the Town Council. Taking place in April, it's a showcase for the finest meat of northern Italy.

Wine cellars in Franciacorta

Franciacorta's superb gastronomic tradition is essentially bipolar and based around meat and fish dishes: traditional peasant meat dishes from central Franciacorta and fish dishes from the lakeside area of Iseo.

Visitors will encounter a mouthwatering assortment of specialties in the local restaurants and delicatessens. Gastro pubs and trattorie serve succulent dishes continuing the tradition of tasty and simple cuisine, focusing on a few local dishes made with local produce.

The renaissance that the traditional wine-making techniques of Franciacorta is currently enjoying has fueled the dawning of a new era in gastronomy, with exceptionally talented chefs recently emerging on the scene.

Franciacorta is one of the few areas north of the Apennines that enjoys an adequately mild climate propitious for the cultivation of the olive tree to produce the Laghi Lombardi extra virgin olive oil – Sebino. Polenta made with stone ground maize is a staple of the local diet and is traditionally eaten with meat, fish or cheese. Butter and cheese can be melted into it or it can be mixed with a ragù sauce or cut into fine slices and fried or grilled. Ravioli and casonsei, bite sized pasta stuffed with a variety of fillings are very popular. Luertis (also referred to as lovertis), is a little known wild growing hop used to enhance the flavor of risotti and frittate.

The fish caught in Lake Iseo is highly prized, in particular whitefish, perch, twaite shad and tench. Oven baked stuffed Tench served with polenta is a specialty of the Clusane d'Iseo riviera. The freshwater tiny allis shads are traditionally left to dry in the sun and then preserved in olive oil. They are also eaten grilled, brushed with olive oil and served with polenta.

Wild mushrooms, including porcini and chanterelles that proliferate on the spurs of the Alps, are delicious in frittate, risotti, and pasta dishes and stews. The salame of Monte Isola, not only the largest island in Lake Iseo but also in Europe, is highly sought after, despite its limited production.

Beef has always featured heavily in the local diet, so much so that manzo all'olio is Franciacorta's signature dish – its first documented recipe dates from as early as 1500. The recipe comes from Rovato, whose inns were famed for their boiled meat and tripe dishes.

Tench

Pork skewers made with farmyard reared meat are festive fare for the townspeople of Brescia. Fowl is used widely in the local cuisine. Restaurants by law can only use imported frozen fowl, and it is only in private houses that you can still sample locally shot fowl.

A wide selection of cheeses are made in Franciacorta, many of which are made according to time-honored traditions and bear the DOP classification. Try Brescia's Robiola lightly brushed with olive oil, or Salva and Silter, delicious eaten with honey or sweet mustards. Try the flavoursome Taleggio dop or the famous Grana Padano dop, Provolone Valpadana dop, Quartirolo dop and Gorgonzola dop.

Where to eat in Iseo:

Restaurants in Iseo:

- Rosa Via Roma 47, +39 030 980 053 All ingredients are top-choice and you may choose local fish from the Iseo-lake or seafood prepared in simple but elegant ways. High ranking in my top-ten.

- Le Margherite Via Risorgimento 251, Clusane sul Lago, +39 030 982 9205 Starters very good .. first superlatives, amazing desserts !!! The portions are generous and the kindness of the staff makes you want to come back soon. The environment is very stylish, clean, style a bit 'retro, but very enjoyable!

- Osteria Pane al Sale Corte Filanda Pirola 6 | Clusane sul Lago, +39 030 989174 With a view on the Iseo lake, you can here enjoy a very tastefull italian menu with local products and some wines of the area. Discreet but efficient service and a calm down place for a romantic dinner.

- I due Roccoli via Bonomelli, +39 030 982 2977 This restaurant is in a beautiful setting with a gorgeous view on the Lake of Iseo. Fantastic offer for sparkling wines from Franciacorta. Good restaurant with great service and interesting menus.

- Ristoran te pizzeria bocconcino Via Ponta 25-27 | Clusane d'Iseo, +39 030 989 497 The place includes a beautiful backyard. Service and food are great. The decoration tastefully done, giving the place a homy feeling.

- Locanda dei Borghesi Vicolo delle Cantine 8, +39 340 393 1785 A great little spot which is easy to overlook. Down a tiny alley with a few tables outside but surprisingly hard to get into. Must book on the weekend as its obviously popular with the locals.

- Restaurant Bella Iseo Via Fenice 4, +39 030 986 8537 Great views over the lake, it's just by the lake! Attentive, kind and helpful service, waitress really great. Great food.

Brescia

Old and New Cathedral

At Iseo (13 miles from Pisogne), we take the road which, some 11 miles later, brings us to Brescia, where we can spend one day visit.

The ancient city of Brixia, Brescia has been an important regional center since pre-Roman times and a number of Roman and medieval monuments are preserved, among which is the prominent castle.

The city is at the center of the third-largest Italian industrial area, concentrating on mechanical and automotive engineering and machine tools. Its companies are typically small or medium- sized enterprises, often with family managements. The financial sector is also a major employer, and the tourist industry is important as well, given the proximity of Lake Garda, Lake Iseo and the Alps.

The city was awarded a Gold Medal for its resistance against Fascism, in the late World War II.

On May 28, 1974, it was the seat of the bloody Piazza della Loggia bombing

Piazza della Loggia

The city of Brescia is the administrative capital of the Province of Brescia, one of the largest in Italy, with over 1,200,000 Inhabitants.

Founded over 3,200 years ago, Brescia (Brixia in antiquity) has Been an important regional center since pre-Roman times. Its old town contains the best-preserved Roman public buildings in northern Italy and Numerous monuments, These Among the medieval castle, the Old and New cathedral, the Renaissance Piazza della Loggia and the rationalist Victory Square.

The monumental archaeological area of the Roman Forum and the monastic complex of San Salvatore-Santa Giulia have become a UNESCO World Heritage Site as part of a group of seven inscribed as Longobards in Italy. Places of the power (568-774 Ceo.).

The city is at the center of the third-largest Italian industrial area, concentrating on mechanical and automotive engineering and machine tools, as well as Beretta and Fabarm firearm manufacturers.

Nicknamed the Lioness of Italy ("Lioness of Italy"), Brescia is known for being the original production area of the Franciacorta wine and for the prestigious Mille Miglia car race That starts and ends in this city. In Additions, Brescia is the setting for most of the action in Manzoni's Adelchi.

Main sights

- **Piazza della Loggia**, an noteworthy example of Renaissance *piazza*, with the synonymous loggia built in 1492 by the architect Filippino de' Grassi.

- The **Duomo Vecchio** ("Old Cathedral"), erected in the 11th century and containing works by Palma the Younger, Alessandro Bonvicino, Romanino and others.

- The **Duomo Nuovo** ("New Cathedral"). The main attractions is the Arch of Sts. Apollonius and Filastrius (1510).

- The **Broletto**, formerly the Town Hall.

- In Piazza del Foro is the most important array of Roman remains in Lombardy. These include the **Capitoline Temple**, built by Vespasianus in 73 CE.

- The **Basilica of San Salvatore**, dating from the Lombard age but later renovated several times. It is one of the best example of High Middle Ages architecture in northern Italy.

- **Santa Maria dei Miracoli**, with a fine facade decorated with bas-reliefs and a Renaissance *peristilium*.

- The Romanesque-Gothic church of **St. Francis**.

Where to eat in Brescia:

Restaurants in Brescia:

- La Piazzetta Via Indipendenza, 87c | Rione San Eufemia, +39 030 362 668 Welcoming and elegant. Elegant table, excellent food with top-quality ingredients. If you don't like to be deceived by arty swooshs painted on your plate with some kind of sauce this is your place! the quiet atmosphere at lunchtime invited to stay and enjoy a glass of caribbean rum.

- Agora Caffe Via dei Musei 75, +39 327 677 9536 A small bar/restaurant - maybe 20 covers. For such a small place the menu is very extensive. Also the range of vegetarian choices is quite wide.

- Osteria Vecchio Botticino Piazzale Arnaldo, 6, +39 030 637 1830 This is how italy once was and should be. A lovely family owned Osteria where italians bring their families. Andrea our host took care of us with the utmost attention and made us feel at home. The mother of Andrea is the creator of the menu and excells in the small kitchen She takes care of the general outline as well as lovely details like the tasty bread from Sardinia. The place is well worth the 12 min walk east of the doumo. Book by phone.

- Ristorante Castello Malvezzi Via Colle S. Giuseppe 1, +39 030 200 4224 Where to start? Just wonderful in every department! Located high over the magical city of Brescia, about 20 euros in a taxi from the centre, the old and lovingly restored building sprawls over the hillside with gardens, terraces, dining rooms and lounges all achingly beautiful and crying out to be enjoyed.

- Il Lorenzaccio Via Cipro 78, +39 030 220 457 Il Lorenzaccio is a nice little restaurant in an unassuming location. The ambience is very cosy, more resembling a living room than a restaurant. The menu features hearty Italian cuisine with a twist, but at moderate prices. Everything is very nice. The service competent and very friendly English menus are available upon request.

Lake Garda

We leave Brescia by taking Viale Venezia in the direction of Lake Garda, the largest of the Italian lakes. After 15 miles, we reach Desenzano and by keeping to the shore of the lake, end up at the gentle peninsula on which stands the many-towered town of Sirmione, with its handsome Scaliger Castle, as welt as several important Roman ruins. At SIRMIONE, we will spend the night, we have the option of spending one additional day without car on the boat on the Lake Garda, and then leaving the next morning, by way of Peschiera, for MANTUA.

Desenzano

Desenzano – Photo © sergiosdaily

A dynamic and lively town, rich in memories and activities, **Desenzano** is the ideal place for a holiday which is a perfect balance between relaxation and fun, nature and culture: thanks to its easy access and its geographical position, it is one of the easiest destinations to reach, the ideal departure point for your next holiday on Lake Garda.

Desenzano and Lake Garda: in the heart and in the history of Europe, where customs and cultures meet and blend together. A famous Riviera, set between the Alpine snows and the Mediterranean sun, caressed by a unique, mild climate all year round.

This land, which was formed by thousands of years of glacial activity, still bears the traces of prehistoric man, of Roman colonization, the passage of the Celts and the Venetian culture, of France and of Central Europe.

Time stood still on the shores of the lake and has fixed memories and emotions of a past which is recalled every day in the works of art, in the rich museums, in the precious monuments on the corners of the streets of Desenzano.

Roman remains, Middle-age fortresses, old parish churches and Renaissance paintings frame a center which is rich in history, art and culture.

Important confirmation of the most important historical eras can be found in Desenzano, starting with the Civic Archaeological Museum, which houses a plough from 2000 B.C. (the oldest to be found to date), the Roman Villa with its mosaic floors and the relics housed in the Antiquarium.

The Castle, from the High Middle Ages, and the Cathedral, which houses some precious paintings, such as Tiepolo's "Last Supper", are both very interesting.

The Port of Desenzano

Old Port – Photo © DonnyJ

The Republic of Venice established itself permanently in the Garda region and in the territories of Brescia and Bergamo after the peace of Lodi in 1454. During this time the port of Desenzano was completely renovated. However the outer breakwater, up to the lighthouse with its lantern, date back to the nineteenth century.

Before the nineteenth century the small port (nowadays known as the Old Port) was protected by a large quay and by some rocks which curbed the force of the waters when the lake was stormy, boats could also be moored to the quay opposite the port.

The traffic of goods in the nineteenth century was noteworthy, goods departed from Desenzano or arrived there from other lakeside towns, either on small boats or on larger craft towed by small tugs.

A tramline set out from a small square, which now houses the gardens at the start of the lakeside promenade "C. Battisti", and linked Desenzano to Castiglione and Mantova. The Venetian style bridge which crosses the entrance to the small port was built in this century, in the thirties. The large wet dock to the south was also built in the thirties.

Nowadays the "nineteenth century style" steamboats, with their beautiful slender shape, have all but disappeared, to be replaced by motorboat-ferries and extremely fast hydrofoils.

The Roman Villa

The Roman Villa

The Villa in Desenzano is, nowadays, the most important testimony, in Northern Italy, to the grand and sumptuous ancient villas.

The building, situated just north of the Gallic way, enjoyed an excellent environment and landscape along the southern shores of Lake Garda.

Nowadays anyone who wants to have an idea of the composition of the villa must use their imagination to make the large and distinct blocks of the building, dating from the IV century B.C., emerge from the ruins, but without considering, in this first approach, all those other elements which date back to earlier dwellings, and that can be glimpsed here and there.

So, what can be drawn from these numerous separate ruins is an impression of a complex building, widely spread and characterized by three main areas, a first sector for extravagant stately functions, a second mainly residential area and a third which is for the most part thermal.

At the entrance to the villa there is also a small museum which, in three rooms, exhibits finds from numerous archaeological digs: amongst these there are the remains of some very interesting statues and pictures, as well as a mill for pressing grapes or olives.

The Castle of Desenzano

The castle is the building which characterizes the appearance of the town of Desenzano, either when seen on arrival from inland, or when seen from the port, or even further away, from the lake. At the end of the fifteenth century the castle, which has its origins in the High Middle-Ages and probably stands on the foundations of a Roman castrum, was extended towards the south; however, it never became a military fortress, although the extension was carried out in order to house a garrison. It still continued its major role as a refuge for the population.

Inside the castle there were the private homes of a few citizens which were always ready to accommodate those who lived outside the castle walls in the event of danger. In later years the castle gradually surrendered its function as a refuge, families continued to live there although its deterioration throughout the nineteenth century grew steadily worse.

Desenzano Castle

In the castle there was even a church, the church of St. Ambrose, which was used as a private house. The layout of the castle is that of an irregular rectangle, with a tower rising up at the entrance, on the northern side, protecting the drawbridge, of which the loop-holes for the chains can still be seen today. It is a square-built tower with a single window in the upper part.

In 1882 the castle was used as a barracks, first as the headquarters of an infantry garrison, then for Bersaglieres and finally for the Alpine troops from the thirties until 1943. The old castle, although devoid of any particular architectural beauty, apart from the facade, is undoubtedly of great historical interest and of spectacular charm. All that remains of the old castle are some lengths of defense walls with crumbling catwalks between the four cut-off towers, with the exception of the one on the north-eastern corner which up until 1940 was used as an observatory. From its terrace you can enjoy one of the most beautiful views of Lake Garda.

Where to eat in Desenzano

Restaurants in Desenzano:

- Ristorante Esplanade Via Lario 3, +39 030 914 3361 Very elegant setting of this beautiful Restaurant building giving directly on the lake. The restaurant is located in the quiter part of Desenzano. The friendliness of the owner and the staff are very promising and only underline the excellent food creations that are offered.

- Pizzeria Vesuvio Via Mezzocolle, 37, +39 030 914 0092 English not spoken here. Who needs it... Ciro, owner and pizza maker, knows rudimentary English and the rest is hand gestures and pointing, and it works great. Fresh dough, thin crust, local salami, recently picked bell peppers, yum! Add two beverages and a side of hot and crispy fries (fresh oil) and you are in heaven. Use a GPS or you won't find the place. Minimal seating - counter top and bar stools.

- La Goccia Trattoria Via Montonale Basso, 13, +39 030 910 3194 Notwithstanding that it is out in the country a bit, it is relatively easy to get to because it is only a couple miles off the A4 highway between Venezia and Milano. Note to all - do not try this restaurant without a reservation. This is a place that the locals go and know about and it is always packed. Great seafood, great preparation, and excellent value.

- Pipol Via Roma, 73/B, +39 030 912 7357 Its a beautiful setting. Waiters do speak good English. Food is good, pesto isn't like the American style pesto but it's very good. Outside eating area at the end of the pedestrian walk doesn't look that promising but as night draws on it's more than acceptable.

- Hosteria Croce d'Oro Vittorio Veneto, +39 030 999 1773 There are manly restaurants in Desenzano down by the lake, whereas this restaurant is up the hill a bit off the lake. Food very well prepared and extremely tasty, price-value good. Not only typical Italian dishes but also specialties. The staff is very caring and polite.

Sirmione

Sirmione Castello Scaligero

"Sirmio, jewel of islands and of peninsulas, Whatever each Neptune carries In the stagnant clear waters and in the vast sea, How gladly and how happy I see you, Scarcely myself believing myself that I have left behind Thynia and the Bithynian fields and that I see you in safety. O what is more blessed than cares freed, When the mind puts down its burden, And we tired from foreign labor come To our hearth and rest in a longed for bed? This is that which is the one thing for such great labors. Greetings, O beautiful Sirmio, and rejoice in your master rejoicing; And you, O Lydian waves of the lake, Laugh whatever there is of laughter at home." (Catullus)

the verses of Catullus roll like waves: he loved and sang of Sirmione as "the gem of all the peninsulas".

The details have faded away in the wake of time, but the Roman poet's spirit still lives in Catullus' Villa and Catullus' Grotte, the original purpose of which is a secret of lake Garda.

The eventful history of the Peninsula has had many highs and lows, but Sirmione never lost its magic.

Be they Romans or Cimbrians, Goths or Avars, Scaligers or Venetians, all where touched by its fabulous charm.

The island just out on Lake Garda like an arm and the water mirrors its luminous image.

Not only Catullus, but also Caesaris is said to have stayed here. In the 8th Century, the Longobards built a convent, Dante came looking for inspiration, Carducci and Boito spent meaningful hours here.....

The Romans built two castles, two harbors, a settlement and the gigantic villa that rises on rocks and powerfully towers on the lake. On the foundations of the old eastern harbor, the Scaligers later built their famous fortress: a charming, graceful yet strong and imposing catwalk, one of the most beautiful buildings in the word.

The numerous villas, churches such as Santa Maria Maggiore's and San Pietro in Mavino's, the wonderful frescoes, unique portals, belfries, battlements, arches and columns, the hamlets of Lugana and Colombare, which like inviting gardens lead to the center of the town, all are slats of the fan known as Sirmione.

Sirmione, however, is something more.....

Sirmione, spa and resort, spirit and culture, restaurants and refined discotheques, thermal baths and outstanding hotels, gastronomy and pizza, excellent wine, markets and fashion shops, the International Academy for Literature, Luna park and Gardaland – a child's paradise – the meeting point of tradition and future.

Here one finds and meets others. Sirmione is simple and complex, young and old, full of life and movement but also silent and contemplative, the Eldorado of water sports and a dreamy village in the twilight. Contrasts. Sirmione is like a fan with many slats, but it remains unique in its essence.

Sirmione Castle

Sirmione – a forum for conferences and for exchanging ideas – a place for sports, active live, rest, a place of wine, silence, culture. A symphony of leisure, tradition and health.

Sirmione where contrasts meet…..

An ideal location. Which other place is free from through traffic and yet linked to the main motorways? Sirmione. Just look around you.

Where to eat in Sirmione

Restaurants in Sirmione:

- Trattoria Clementina Piazza Rovizzi, 13, +39 030 919 6663 The place is not very easy to find and its very small, during the weekend make a reservation. However, the food, fish, is good. A simple but very delicious fish. The food is really tasty and the staff very friendly (they speak perfect German, as well as quite fluent English). Not much to chose from from the menu but that way you know you're getting fresh and really homecooked food.

- Ristorante L'Incontro Via Colombare N 31 | Piazza Campiello, +39 030 990 5409 It is a refined and elegant, with a wonderful terrace overlooking the lake, surrounded by a beautiful garden. I find it very suitable for receptions class. The service is accurate, attentive, professional. The menu is simple and does not have a lot of dishes, but there are always delicious food. Average prices of course also important rapportati location. I recommend it for romantic dates, convivial dinners and lunches, special events and receptions

- Ristorante Risorgimento Piazza Carducci, 5/6 +39 030 916325 The menu is a good range of meat and fish dishes with a good choice of sides. The service is outstanding, professional and attentive but not intrusive. The staff friendly and genuinely seems to be enjoying their work and happy to be delivering a great customer experience.

- Quanto Basta Via Colombare, 96, +39 030 9905037 Not the traditional Italian fare offered in most restaurants, and priced slightly more also, but totally worth it. This place is gorgeous and seems to be popular with Italians (which is always good) Great experience, fabulous food and good customer service.

- La Rucola Vicolo Strentelle, 7, +39 030 916326 Don't go to La Rucola if you are looking for an traditional Italian meal. Although right in the middle of the postcard-like old town of Sirmione, This trendy place filled with modern art has some local touch but serves sophisticated fusion food with a strong Asian flavor. The 80€ discovery menu is a great way to sample the chef's own way of cooking: super fresh ingredients (lots of seafood), a strong attention for design (both the dishes and the dining ware) and distinctive spices. The friendly and professional staff provides excellent service without overdoing it. Not cheap of course but worth it for a refined gastronomic dinner.

Mantova

Mantova palazzo Ducale

This extraordinary city, founded perhaps by the Etruscans, was then Romanized (Vergil was born in nearby Andes) and finally, after a period as a commune, became a fief of the Bonacolsi and then of the Gonzagas (1328-1707), who made it the splendid capital of their principality. The River Mincio closes it on three sides in the form of a lake, and to those approaching it from the north, the city presents a striking skyline of towers.

We enter by Porta Molina, turn down Via Trento, where the handsome Palazzo Cavriani may be seen, cross Piazza Virgiliana and, passing alongside the tall Torre della Gabbia, come into Piazza Sordello, an impressive medieval square with the two battlemented palaces, Palazzo Bonacolsi and Palazzo del Capitano, which constitute the old wing of the palatial residence of the Gonzagas, the largest group of buildings in Italy (365.000 sq. ft., with 450 rooms) after the Vatican.

Palazzo Ducale (Gonzaga Palace)

Palazzo Ducale

This complex of buildings is extremely interesting, both for the beauty of the rooms as well as for its art collections. The whole body of buildings, which were erected, enlarged and restructured in different periods (XIII – XVIII century) covers a total area of about 34.000 sq.m., some parts of which stand out distinctly:

- Domus Magna
- Palazzo del Capitano
- Castello di San Giorgio
- Chiesa di Santa Barbara

and a series of courtyards, small squares and gardens.

Palazzo Ducale

The "Captain's Palace," together with the Domus Magna, is the oldest part of the whole complex (1200 A.D.) and an important testament to medieval Mantua architecture.

The two buildings can today be seen on the eastern side of Piazza Sordello.

The Saint George Castle was built between 1300 A.D. and 1400 A.D. to strengthen both the military and political power of the *Gonzaga*, who entrusted its plans to the architect *Bartolino da Novara*.

La camera degli Sposi

Mantova camera degli sposi

In 1459 the building was turned into a residence. Inside, visitors can see the famous "Camera degli Sposi" by *Andrea Mantegna*.

The Church of Saint Barbara, designed by *Giovan Battista Bertani*, was built around the middle of the sixteenth-century.

It houses wooden sculptures dating back to the end of the seventeenth-century, as well as precious sacred vestments.

The Hanging Garden (Giardino Pensile), designed by *P. Pedemonte* and built in 1579, is well worth a visit.

The central nucleus of the political life under the patronage of the House of Gonzaga, Palazzo Ducale also became the center of artistic life.

Among its guests were internationally famous artists such as *Mantegna*, *Pisanello*, *Giulio Romano*, and *Rubens*, who decorated and enriched the various parts of the palace with paintings, frescos, tapestries, statues, decorations and extremely refined furnishings.

Mantegna's fresco, the Gonzaga's court

The Palace, plundered many times in the past, was restored to its original splendor in the present century.

It contains an excellent Archaeological Museum and a painting gallery with works by Pisanello, Tintoretto, El Greco, Rubens, and Van Dvck.

But to be admired most of all is the astonishing succession of rooms, the alternating vast and tiny courtyards, the labyrinthine passageways, the sumptuous galleries and the refinement of the decoration – in short, the elegant setting which still tells us so much about the magnificence of this court, where the first opera in the history of music was conceived and written by Claudio Monteverdi.

Palazzo Te

Mantova Palazzo Te

Behind the palace stands the Castle of S. Giorgio (14th century), later incorporated into it.

After taking a walk around the Castle, we come back into Piazza Sordello, near the 18th century Cathedral and Bishop's Palace, from which we carry on into the square where the ancient Broletto stands (in a niche, a 13th century statue of Vergil), and then into Piazza delle Erbe, with the Palazzo della Ragione and the Rotondo di S. Lorenzo (ca. 1000), the oldest building in the city.

In the nearby Basilica di S. Andrea, designed by L. Battista Alberti (1472), we will find a beautiful Madonna by Lorenzo Costa, two paintings by Mantegna and the Painter's Tomb.

By taking Via Roma and Via Chiassi, we come into Via Prima, where, after the church of San Barnaba, we come upon the Palazzo di Giustizia (formerly Cofloredo) a distinguished 16th century building.

Mantova at night

Then we find the House of Giulio Romano: the masterpiece of this artist, both as an architect and a painter, is, in Mantua, the Palazzo del Te (reached by taking Via Acerbi), an imposing princely villa, perhaps the most beautiful pleasure house of the High Renaissance.

From here we turn towards Viale Risorgimento and Corso Garibaldi, where we find the charming 15th century facade of S. Maria del Gradaro.

Down Via Trieste we come to the picturesque Rio, which we cross; in Via Pomponazzi stands the important Palazzo Sordello not far from which is the Accademia Virgiliana with an 18th century Theatre designed by Bibiena.

Itinerary to visit the old town

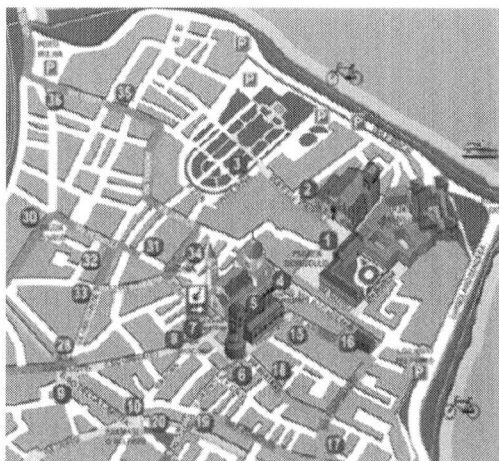

Yellow itinerary

1] Piazza Sordello

This itinerary starts from **Piazza Sordello** which, together with its surroundings, constituted the ancient town, founded upon what was the original island and is still today the heart of the city.

The piazza, dedicated to Mantuan poet Sordello da Goito, mentioned by Dante in the 6th canto of the *Purgatorio,* was created over the course of the 14th century; it was the center of the religious and political scene, where first the *Bonacolsi* and then the *Gonzaga* family built their imposing palaces.

It is rectangular in shape, with the **Cathedral** standing on the north side.

On the east side, to the right looking at the Cathedral, the square is dominated by the two porticoed buildings which make up the facade of the Ducal Palace complex: the *Magna Domus* and the *Palazzo del Capitano.*

San Giorgio Castle

Not far beyond stands the **Castello di San Giorgio**, built by *Francesco Gonzaga*, around the end of the 14th century in order to extend the palace and defend it with a strong bulwark. The building is an imposing fortress built in brickwork on a square plan, with four massive towers at the corners and a moat all around.

Returning to the piazza, opposite the Ducal Palace stands the **Bishop's Palace** and several adjoining historic family mansions: the **Uberti Palace**, the **Castiglioni Palace** and the **Acerbi Palace**.

The **Bishop's Palace** was built between 1776 and 1786 and belonged to the *Marchesi* Bianchi family who lived in it until 1823 when it was turned into the bishop's seat. On the facade, two impressive telamons at the sides of the entrance support a marble balcony.

At the corner with vicolo Bonacolsi, stands the late gothic **Uberti Palace**, built by a Mantuan branch of the Florentine family from which it takes its name. Traces of the original 13th century structures are still visible, partly walled up during later reconstructions, especially the windows facing vicolo Bonacolsi.

Next is **Castiglioni Palace**, otherwise known as **Bonacolsi Palace**, as it was believed to be the home of the Bonacolsi family, built by Pinamonte in 1281; it was more likely built by *Luigi Gonzaga* after he took over the town, in around 1340. Since 1808 it has been property of the Castiglione family, descendants of the famous Baldassare, author of *Il Cortegiano (The Book of the Courtier).* The vast facade in brickwork is crowned by Ghibelline merlons; on the upper floor are three-mullioned windows in terracotta and white marble. On the lower floor is a series of single lancet windows, nowadays almost all bricked in. On the ground floor to the far left side, the original entrance, topped by a pointed arch, bears the Bonacolsi family coat of arms. The present entrance door and the balcony are 18th century additions. The tower facing vicolo Bonacolsi is also part of this complex.

Tower of the Cage

Next to the Castiglioni Palace, stands the **Acerbi Palace**, one of the Bonacolsi family mansions, with the adjoining **Tower of the Cage,** the tallest tower in town. It gained this name in 1576 when *Guglielmo Gonzaga* had an iron cage placed on it which was used to imprison criminals.

2] Seminary

A few meters from the Cathedral, along via Cairoli, stands the **Seminary**. Its neo-classical facade was built in 1825 from designs by *Giovan Battista Vergani*.

3] Piazza Virgiliana

Piazza Virgiliana

Walking along via Cairoli, one reaches **Piazza Virgiliana**. The piazza was once an inlet of the *Lago di Mezzo* (Middle Lake), filled in between the mid-18th and the beginning of the 19th century. The square was created from a project by *Paolo Pozzo* and dedicated t o *Virgil*. The Neo-classical look still remains in a few of the buildings around it, although it was radically altered when it became a park during the 1930s. The Virgil monument was inaugurated in 1927: it was designed by architect *Luca Beltrami*, the bronze statue of Virgil is by *Emilio Quadrelli*, while the marble sculptures at the sides are by *Giuseppe Mengozzi*.

From via Cairoli, going left, is the **Diocesan Museum of Sacred Art "Francesco Gonzaga"** where precious works of art dating back to the time of the Gonzaga family are on display; not to be missed are the suits of armor, once housed at the *Sanctuary of Santa Maria delle Grazie*, made by the famous Missaglia armorists.

4] Piazza Broletto

Renaissance Porticos

The itinerary continues to **Piazza Broletto**, walking past the **Voltone di San Pietro**, the archway of the old town gate.

Once past it, the **Renaissance porticos** begin, supported by columns with capitals of different periods and coming from different places. At this point, one reaches Piazza Broletto, created at the end of the 12th century when the town was extended beyond the first set of walls.

The square is dominated by buildings dating back to the time of the Commune, such as the **Palazzo del Podesta'**. It was built in

1227, as an inscription on the facade explains, as seat of the town government, which was ruled by the *Podesta'*. The building was partially destroyed by several fires and was later rebuilt, with many alterations. The internal courtyard, reached by walking through the **Sottoportico dei Lattonai** has a charming late Gothic staircase that leads to the upper floor.

On the facade facing piazza Broletto the **Edicola di Virgilio** can be seen; according to tradition the statue set in the niche represents the poet Virgil seated on an academic's chair and dressed as a medieval doctor with the typical cap.

To the left stands the vast round arch of the **Arengario**, built around 1300 to connect the *Palazzo del Podesta'* to the **Masseria**, where once all financial transactions took place. Above the arch are two elegant three-mullioned windows and a *loggetta*. From there the rulings of the Commune magistrates were announced to the people. Under the vast arch, four iron rings are still visible which served to hang the ropes used for those condemned to receive "*squassi di corda*" (the torture of being shaken on ropes).

5] Piazza Erbe - Palazzo della Ragione

Palazzo della Ragione

Continuing along the porticos one reaches **Piazza Erbe**, so-called because it is here that the vegetable and fruit market takes place. It is dominated by the **Palazzo della Ragione** and the adjoining **Clock Tower**. The tower was built in 1472 from a design by *Luca Fancelli*; in 1573 the astrological and astronomical clock created by *Bartolomeo Manfredi* was added to the tower; in the niche under the clock, there is a statue of the *Immaculate Conception* dated 1639.

Next to the tower rises the **Rotonda di San Lorenzo**, the oldest church in town.

6] Piazza Concordia

Casa di Boniforte

Behind the Rotonda, is **Piazza Concordia**. To the left, in via Spagnoli, is the **Chamber of Commerce**, an interesting building in Liberty style designed by the Mantuan architect *Aldo Andreani* at the beginning of the 20th century.

Returning to Piazza Erbe, to the right on the south side, one can see the **Casa di Boniforte** (so-called **House of the Merchant**), as it was built in 1455 by a wealthy merchant – *Giovanni Boniforte da Concorezzo*; the building has an exceptional facade with an interesting mix of various ornamental motifs; the small portico is supported by Corinthian columns. Adjoining the house is the **Torre del Salaro**, built in the 13th century and later used as a deposit for salt.

7] Piazza Mantegna

Piazza Mantegna

Adjacent to Piazza Erbe is **Piazza Mantegna**, dominated by the solemn facade of the **Basilica di Sant'Andrea**. It is the largest church in town, worthy of a visit as it houses important works of art.

Where to eat in Mantua

Restaurants in Mantova:

- *Carlo Govi* restaurant - Viale Gorizia 13/B, Mantua +39 0376 355 133: The restaurant is located in a residential neighbourhood outside the historical centre of Mantua, in a spotless and stylish setting. Overall Carlo Govi is arguably as good as less than 50 Euro (provided you don't exceed with wine) can get you, not only in Mantua, but in most Italian cities.

- *Taverna Cinquecento* restaurant - Via Bertani 78, Mantua +39 339 267 0007: This place has a selected offer of dishes, but you can bet that what you are going to taste will satisfy your mouth. Good choices of wine that will be your best friend for the evening. They have also a fantastic raindeer if you woul like to try something special not really local but amazing.

- *Lo Scalco Grasso* restaurant - Via Trieste 55, Mantua +39 349 374 7958: Great dinner, prices balanced, even glasses of wine available. Large choices of different kind of food: meat or fish. It is worth to try the experience of this Osteria: Rely on the gentle and expert waiters about the choice of the dishes suggested from them time to time. Environment also refined.
  The place is often full booked. This is an evidence about the good food and the correct prices. Reservations are required even during the week.

- *Zzino Tramezzino* sandwiches - Corso Della Liberta 7, Mantua +39 346 660 6413: Excellent quality for a fair price. This restaurant opened recently, and it will not dissapoint you. There are really a lot of options "small sandwiches" (tramezzini) to choose from and they suggest they can prepare one custom if you like.

- *La Piadineria* piadine (sandwiches) - Giovanni Battista Spagnoli, 18, Mantua +39 0376 288 231: Amazing place to drop by and eat something, nice staff, good prices, some tables to sit, wifi. very central location

- *La Maison Du Chocolat et...* chocolate and gelato - Via Oberdan 8, Mantua +39 0376 321 081: It is the place for those who love chocolate. Taste the hot chocolate and you will find it really exquisite. Even the ice creams are very good!

- *Gelateria Pappa Reale* gelato -via Chiassi 89, Mantua +39 349 127 8418: They don't use sugar but their own production honey. If you're looking for 1000 different flavors to choose from, this is not your place. But it is if you look for excellent quality, go for it.

- *Il Gallone - Cocktail & Wine Bar* you can also eat - Via Leon d'Oro 13, Mantua +39 333 433 4682: Some complex and excellent cocktails at affordable prices (6-8euro). Things you may not find back home. Try the smokey ones or the molecular ones - with bubbles of liquors in your glass. Very friendly bartender who is obviously passionated about the job.

Verona

The Arena

We leave Mantua by the Porta Manin, taking the road which, after 25 miles, brings us to VERONA.

With its position between the banks of the River Adige winding at the foot of the hills, the beauty of its colors, the green of its cypresses, the dark red of its bricks, the ivory of its stone, the white marbles, the extraordinary barroom; of its mixture of Roman, medieval and Renaissance art, and the magnificent splendor of its churches, Verona is one of the most fascinating cities of Italy. An ancient prehistoric settlement, then a city of the Gauls and the Romans, a capital of Ostrogoth, Longobard, and Frankish dynasties, it next passed, after the age of the communes, into the brief, but happy, possession of the Scaligers (1260-1387) and lastly to the Venetian Republic.

Our visit begins in the spectacular Piazza Bra, the site of the enormous Roman Arena (1st century), the largest structure of its kind after the Colosseum.

Next to the Arena, we find the neoclassical Palazzo Municipale. (Town Hall) and, set against the city walls, the Palazzo della Gran Guardia (1610).

Palazzo della Gran Guardia

The palace served as the headquarters and registered office of the city guard and was built in 1610.

The loggia and the parade ground on the ground floor of the palace were designed by Domenico Curtoni. The staircase and upper floor were not completed until 1850. You can see the style of the master builder of Curtoni, Sanmicheli, especially when looking at the twin pillars on the upper floor – they imitate Sanmicheli's Porta Palio.

Today, the former city guard is used as a conference centre and as a gallery.

Passing through the 15th century archways which span Corso Ports Nooks, we come upon the Museum of Gems and Jewelry, with a handsome classical courtyard; beyond Via Roma is a row of three fine palaces, Vaccari, Barbaro and Malfatti (designed by Sammicheli, 1555).

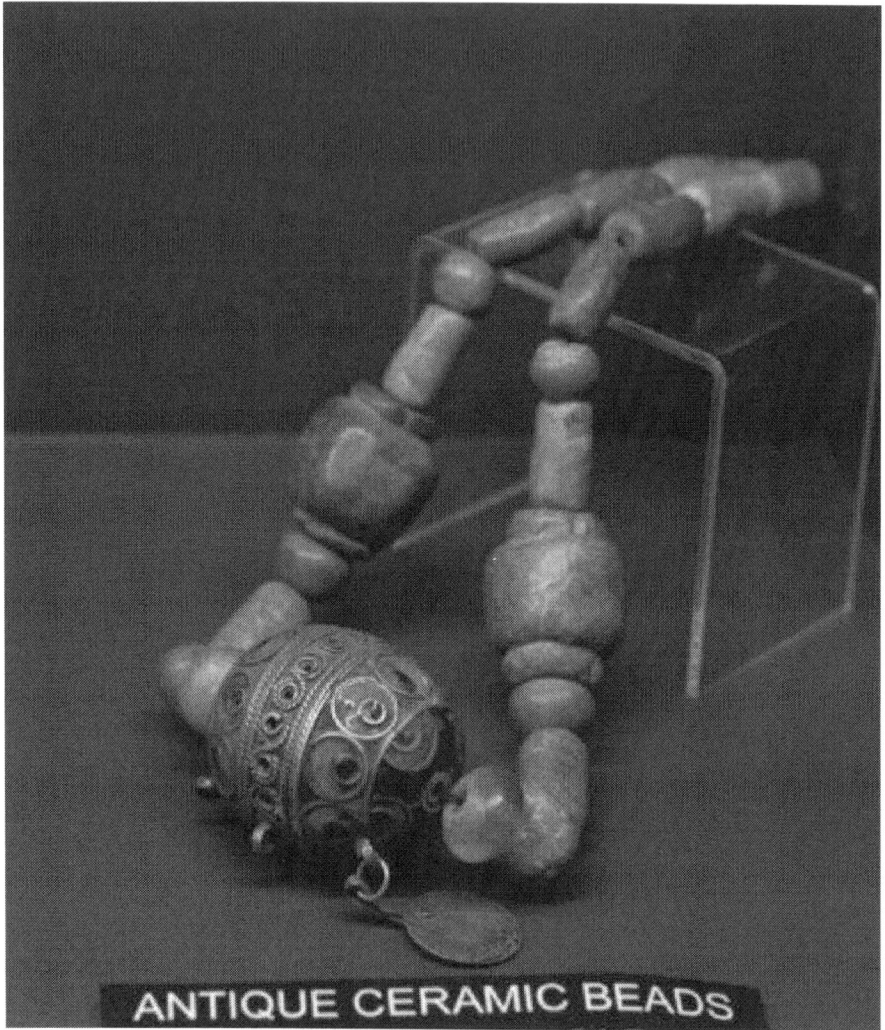

ANTIQUE CERAMIC BEADS

Museum of Gems and Jewelry

Taking Via Roma, we reach Castelvecchio, an impressive 14th century fortress on the Adige, which today houses the Civic Museum and its important collection of Venetian painting (works by G. Bellini, Crivelti, Tintoretto, Titian, Tiepolo, Guardi, and by those gentlest of Veronese artists, Stefano da Zesio and Altichicro).

Before leaving the Castle, we should wander among its towers and battlements to enjoy the marvelous view.

San Bernardino

Taking Stradone Antonio Procolo, we pass by the Renaissance church of San Bernardino (1466), and come to San Zero, the most beautiful church in Verona and one of the most important in Italy. It was founded in the 5th century, but in its present form it dates from 1138, at which time the magnificent face was finished with its elegant porch and carvings by Nicola and Guglielmo, a masterpiece of Romanesque sculpture.

Passing through the superb Romanesque bronze doors, we enter the grandiose interior where, on the high altar, there is a Triptych by Andrea Mantegna (1459), one of the noblest paintings of the Renaissance.

Following the Adige back to Castelvecchio, we go on by it to the superb Arco dei Gavi (ca. 50 AD.), demolished in 1805 by the French and later rebuilt. After the Palazzo Canossa, designed by Sammicheli, we go on down Corso favor where we find, on the left, the Romanesque church of S. Lorenzo, and on the right, the Palazzo Bevilacqua (1530) and the church of SS. Apostoli.

Torre del Gardello

Beyond the Roman Ports Borsari, we come to the Torre del Gardello, in front of which we find the lively Piazza delle Erbe, whence we pass into the adjoining Piazza dei Signori, a superb creation dating from the Middle Ages (Palazzo della Ragione, 1193, and the 13th century Palazzo degli Scaligeri) and from the Renaissance (the splendid Loggia).

Close by here is one of the most enchanting spots in Verona, that stretch of street dominated by the Arche Scaligere, in which, between their palace and S. Maria Antics are buried the Scaliger lords, under whose rule Verona passed out of the Middle Ages into its glorious a Rebirth.

Wandering through the neighboring streets, we come to Juliet's House; then taking Via Stella, we pass be side the 14th century church of S. Maria delta Scala, and then along Via Anfiteatro, with the Palazzo dei Diamanti, we return to Piazza Bra, where we may interrupt our tour for lunch in one of the excellent restaurants.

San Fermo Maggiore

In the afternoon, we start off again from Piazza Bra and going to the left of the Town Hall, reach the very ancient church of San Pietro Incarnario and then San Fermo Maggiore (1261), richly decorated inside with frescoes by Altichievo and with magnificent tombs. From San Fermo, we cross the Adige on the Prime Navi, beyond which is the handsome Palazzo Pompei (1530) designed by Sammicheli, and then the Church of San Paolo (inside, canvases by Veronese, Caroto, etc.).

North of Via Venti Settembre is the church of SS Nazaro and Celso (fine Venetian paintings), from which we make our way to S.

Maria in Organo, an 8th century Benedictine abbey remodeled by Sammicheli (superb inlaid woodwork in the choir dating from 1499).

Passing Santa Chiara (15th century) on our right, we reach the foot of St. Peter's Hill, into the side of which is set the Roman Theatre, in a magnificent position overlooking the city and the curving sweep of the Adige. Nest to it is the Archaeological Museum.

San Giorgio

Following the curve of the Adige, we come to the stately church of San Giorgio (1477-1536) which contains several famous paintings, amongst them the Martyrdom of St. George, a masterpiece by Veronese, and the Baptism of Christ by Tintoretto.

Crossing the bridge in front of the Roman Theatre, only a few steps away we find the Romanesque Cathedral with its lovely semicircular apse (12th century) and a Cloister with small red marble columns; inside, the Assumption by Titian (1540). We then take Via Damon and come to the last masterpiece of Veronese architecture which remains to be seen, Sant'Anastasia, a

Dominican Gothic church (1290) with priceless frescoes by Pisanello.

Porta Borsari

Verona has a ancient historic center, very extensive and well conserved. Roman municipality of the 49 B.C., reserves important tracks of that prosperous period. The roman amphitheater called the Arena, one of the most famous outdoor theatre in the world, the Roman Theatre, the Gavi Arch and the monumental gates (Porta Borsari and the Porta dei Leoni) are grand works designed to last millennia.

Noteworthy architectural works remain from the Scaliger's Seigniory and from the Austrian domination during the

Risorgimento, but there are also, palaces and squares of every epoch and style in warm soft colors.

Verona

The churches of the town are numberless and of great historical and artistic value. Some of the most important are: the Basilica of San Zeno, a perfect example of Romanesque architecture, is dedicated at the Saint Patron of the town and the panels of bronze that adorned the wooden doors, are a work of the local sculpture.

The churches of San Fermo, Santi Apostoli and San Lorenzo date back to the same period while the church of Sant'Anastasia was built during the the Scaligers' Seignory and is the home of fresco masterpieces by Pisanello and Altichiero. The church of San Giorgio is attributed to Sanmicheli, an architect who worked at several of the most important palaces and fortresses of the city.

A small marble balcony records the most famous verses of Shakespeare tragedy, in which Romeo declares his love for Juliet, Shakespeare's immortal heroine, as she stands on it. The building, which probably dates back to the XIII century, has a brick facade and large tribolate windows; following the tradition it is the house where the beautiful Juliet lived. Her tomb is located instead in an old monastery and the place is imbued with an intensely romantic atmosphere.

Juliet Balcony

The other eternal symbol of Verona is the Arena: the magnificence of the roman ruins, the perfection of the staging and the musical shows give to the performances of the Arena that inimitable tone which since 1913 has been attracting big crowds of spectators to one of the most prestigious opera seasons.

Every year the rich program includes works, concerts and ballets. Verona offers also many folklore events between which the "Bacanal del Gnoco", the Veronese carnival, arrived at the 475^ edition.

Where to eat in Verona

Restaurants in Verona:

- <u>La Bottega della Gina</u> Via Fama 4/c, +39 045 594725 Great "fast food" place with handmade art like pasta! Besides tortellini it also serves other pasta and different lunch dishes. Small , not very fussy place, but not only the food is great, but you can also see it done before your eyes.

- <u>Borsari 36</u> Corso Porta Borsari, 36, +39 045 590566 The restaurant is hidden in a small courtyard at Corso Porta Borsari 36. The service and knowledge of the Maitre D is good. The caring service includes the allergies code in case you want to know and they will cook accordingly to you need. The wine list is so extensive and is thick like a bible. The presentation of food is nice and serve with a complimentary starter, sorbet and petit four at the end. Price is reasonable.

- <u>Ghiotto Take Away</u> Via C. Abba 13/g +39 340 079 2112 The couple that runs the place are one of the most warm-hearted, good-humored people you'd ever meet in Verona, you step into their tiny domain to grab a bite and end up finding out the story of their lives, the next thing you know, you're sharing a laugh and indulging yourself with pizza. Believe it or not, the food is just as good, one would never guess that vegan food can be so exciting in its simplicity, super delicious and even kind of inventive. You should definitely come for good food and great company. They've been opened just about few months or so and (no surprise there) have already become a hit. They bake with inspiration and gib heart, trust me, it shows.

- <u>La Griglia</u> Via Leoncino, 29, +39 045 8031212 This restaurant is a trattoria so the interiors have typical Italian rustic charm and the food is simpler in presentation but everything is good and service friendly and warm. The location is actually just behind the Verona roman amphitheatre, Arena di Verona, on the other side away from Piazza Bra. It's just a few steps away from where they place the Aida sets before the Opera season. It looks further than it really is on google maps and you can walk a shorter way if you know where it is. The easier way is to head to the entrance of the Arena, walk around along its perimeter in an anticlockwise direction and look out for Via Leoncino, somewhere on the right.

- Osteria Barucchi via Giacomo Barucchi 88, +39 339 624 6509 Well-managed and well-stocked Osteria, with the chance to taste in peace and quiet tranquility wine and a variety of craft beers and cold cuts and cheeses with fine details. Music in the evening and several events are organized around the time of the year by the owner very nice and well prepared. Recommend also for aperitif and after dinner.

- Antica Torretta Piazza Broilo 1, +39 045 80.15.292 Fantastic flavors and ingredients produce a great experience in an elegant indoor setting. Nestled in a quiet part of Verona with some of the most attentive waitstaff present is a great place to bring someone you love. The chef makes the effort to entice you with his creativity. The portions are small but of the highest quality. Each bite is savored as an individual experience. The wine list is excellent as well.

- Nastro Azzurro Vicolo Listone 4, +39 045 8004457 Pizza served outside in an atmospheric setting just off the Piazza Bra. Really tasty pizza, attentive, efficient staff. Though not in the piazza, but in a side street on the edge of it, the location is a delight, particularly if you reserve a table with a view of the Arena. The food is good and the menu varied. However what makes the difference is the service. The staff are friendly, knowledgeable and efficient. they seem to be just as happy to serve a quick pizza or a more fancy meal.

- Enoteca Segreta Vicolo Samaritana, +39 045 801 5824 out of the way but not too far off the main piazza Erbe, this place has a nice outside courtyard as well as an atmospheric cellar like inside. Food is beautiful, service friendly and very reasonable. Don't miss the dessert. It's nicely tucked away at the end of a tiny, out of the way street, so there's lots of atmosphere before you even enter. There's a sweet alfresco area on a deck out the front and a cellar downstairs. The place is off the beaten track and apparently very popular with the locals. The food is tasty, wines - great and the atmosphere friendly and perfect for a romantic dinner.

- Trattoria Dal Gal Via Segala Don Gregorio, 39/A, +39 045 890 0966 Leonardo the owner runs an amazing restaurant and has lovingly refurbished it offering the highest quality Italian food and wine with impeccable service. The restaurant is hidden away in a residential area so do not be alarmed that you have taken the wrong road.

- Vecio Macello Via Macello 8, +39 045 803 0348 The fish tasting menu is fabulous. 15 different fish and shellfish to try including an oyster. The tuna is excellent and the scallop adorable. Then just to finish it off you can have a plate of pasta with the ravioli to die for. The house wine for 12 euros is also excellent. The waiting staff is attentive and uses smiles rather than English to make you welcome .

Vicenza

Villa Capra "La Rotonda"

Vicenza, which after evolving historically in much the same way as Verona, blossomed anew under Venice (from 1404). While Verona has a largely medieval aspect, Vicenza appears as a distinctly Renaissance town, mostly due to the efforts of its most important son, Andrea Palladio.

We enter the city, pass the Salvi Gardens (be beyond the gardens, the Loggia Valmarana and the Loggia dei Longhena), through the turreted Ports Castello and find ourselves in Corso Palladio, a fine street cutting Vicenza from one end to the other.

To the left is the Palazzo Bonin (formerly Thiene), designed by Scamozzi; across the way, Palazzo Bizzarri-Malvezzi. Turning left into Corso Fogazzaro, we come to the Franciscan Romanesque-Gothic church of S. Lorenzo, with an interesting doorway and a well-lit interior, its various chapels adorned with ancient frescoes and tombs of San Biagio illustrious citizens.

Following Contra Pedemuro-San Biagio we arrive in Contra Porti, with its magnificent palaces: to the right the Gothic Casa Porto-Scaroni and Palazzo Biego now Porto Festa (1552) designed by Palladio (Inside, frescoes by Tiepolo), and the Venetian-Gothic Palazzo Colleoni-Porto; to the left, Casa Trissino, now Sperotti, restored after air-raid damage in World War II the most beautiful Gothic palace in the town, and the Renaissance palace, Casa Porto, rebuilt after air-raid damage.

Then to the right again, comes Palazzo Thiene, with its terracotta doorway. After this introduction to the architecture of Vicenza, we come into the extraordinary Piazza dei Signori with the famous Basilica, designed by Palladio (1549), the charming Loggia dei Capitanio, also by Palladio, and the long Lombard palace of the Monte di Pieta', which incorporates the Baroque facade of S. Vincenzo.

Two columns support, in the Venetian manner, one a statue of the Saint and the other the Lion of St. Mark, emblem of the Venetian Republic. Passing along one side of the Basilica, we come to Piazza delle Erbe. with its medieval Tower, and then, to Piazza delle Biade, with the Gothic church of S. Maria dei Servi.

We come back and turn right up Corso Palladio (to the left, on the corner is the Gothic Palazzo da Schio) and into Contra Santa Corona, with the Romanesque church of Santa Corona, of brick with an imposing marble doorway. Inside, we see a Baptism of Christ by Giovanni Bellini, an Adoration of the Magi by Veronese and the magnificent Valmarana Chapel by Palladio.

After a short walk we come to two of Palladio's most inspired creations, in the square at the far end of the Corso- The first of these is the Teatro Olimpico, which he began shortly before his death and which was complete roofed by Scamozzi (1583), and which is the first theatre of modern times; and the second is the Palazzo Chiericati (1550), containing the two principal collections of the city: the important Archaeological Collection (with a magnificent Bacchus, of the school of Praxiteles) and the Art Gallery, which contains, besides a fine collection of works by local painters (Montagna, Buonconsigli, Mattei, etc.), some important canvases by Cima da Conegliano, Lotto, Veronese, Bassano, Tintoretto, Van Dyck, the wonderful Diana by Pittoni, pictures by Tiepolo (the

Immacolata) and Piazzetta, and a Flemish masterpiece: Calvary by Hans Memling.

Palazzo Thiene

By way of Via J. Cabianea, we reach Palazzo Godi, designed by Scamozzi (1569), and, from here, the Casa Pigafetta, a magnificent example of florid Gothic architecture, where the famous navigator was born. We then continue down to the Piazaz del Duomo, to the Gothic Cathedral with a dome by Palladio (inside, a Polyptych by L. Veneziano) and to the courtyard of the Bishop's Palace, with its elegant Renaissance Loggia.

Leaving the city, we now climb the hill upon which stands the Basilica di Monte Berice, in order to admire, in the Refectory, a masterpiece by Veronese: The Banquet of Gregory the Great

(1572). Leaving Monte Barico, and turning right, after some 500 yards., we come to the 17th century Villa Valmarana where Tiepolo painted (1757) what is one of the most important series of frescoes of the 18th century. Nearby is the Rotondo, Palladio's most beautiful villa, which has been the model for hundreds of neoclassical buildings in France, England and America.

Leaving Vicenza, and travelling some 14 miles along the foot of Monte Grappa, we reach Cittadella, standing within its marvelous 14th century walls, and after another 7 miles, Castetfranco the birthplace of Giorgione, with its red medieval walls, its Castle, its old painted house and the Cathedral which contains, together with works by Veronese and Bassano, one of Giorgione's masterpieces: a Madonna, painted in 1504.

From Rovigo, after a 23 mile drive over the plain of the Po Delta, we reach the Po, at Pontelagoscuro, and then immediately enter **Ferrara**, well worth one day visit.

Where to eat in Vicenza

Restaurants in Vicenza:

- Ristorante Il Querini da Zemin Viale del sole, 142, +39 0444 552054 To savor the flavors of the traditional local Vicenza food and enjoy delicious combinations on the advice of the professional staff and friendly.

- Il Ceppo Corso Palladio, 196 | Centro Storico Vicenza, +39 0444 544414 This restaurant specialises in baccala. Well cooked and not salty. Pleasant environment, friendly owner who gives you a potted history of the restaurant's links to the baccala' processing business. Slightly cramped but definitely worth a visit and definitely worth the price.

- Trattoria Zamboni via S.Croce, 73 Lapio di Arcugnano, +39 0444.273079 The restaurant is perfect. The atmosphere great. The air very clean. The service personals very kind. Foods extremely delicious.

- Il Molo Contra Pedemuro San Biagio, 48, +39 328 8087598 They don't have a typical menu that you read - the waiters will talk you through the different choices for the courses. Plus you get complimentary water and prosecco!

Treviso in half day

Treviso

TREVISO, in origin a Roman city, then a commune and finally a Venetian possession, mainly medieval in aspect, with picturesque canals and noble buildings.

As soon as we arrive in Treviso, we go straight to San Nicolo a superb Romanesque and Gothic church of refined proportions, the largest in the city, with frescoes by Tomaso da Modena and numerous pictures and sculptures.

From here, by way of Via Battisti and Via S. Liberate, passing the Palladian church of S. Agnese, we reach the Art Gallery, interesting for frescoes by Tomaso da Modena, paintings by Giovanni Bellini, Cima da Conegliano, etc., and works of the 17th and 18th centuries.

Turning down Via Canova (notice the Casa da Noal with its painted facade), we come to the Cathedral, distinguished by its seven domes.

Inside, a tender Annunciation by Titian and the ethereal Madonna dei Fiore by Girolamo da Treviso.

Next to the Cathedral are the 13th century Bishop's Palace and the Baptistery. From here, we walk to the Canale dei Buranelli to see the old houses which line it and finally reach the Piazza dei Signori, the center of the city of Treviso, dominated by the Palazzo dei Trecento (1217) and the Palazzo dei Podesta.

We leave Treviso and head south. Some 4 miles later, we reach Mogliano Veneto, and from here soon come to Mestre (14 miles from Treviso), then 5 miles more, partly on the 19th century bridge over the Lagoon, and we are in VENICE.

Where to eat in Treviso

Restaurants in Treviso:

- Giardino Bistrot Via C. Battisti 35, Bio food cooked in a simple and natural. Tasty and served with fantasy. Ideal for not burdening before returning to the office. The restaurant is very small, but perhaps it is also his most valuable.

- Osteria dalla Gigia Via barberia, 20, +39 0422582752 The best mozzarella in a carriage Triveneto: What a mouth-watering. A wide selection of sandwiches and cicchetti, as was once in the taverns of Treviso. It is located in the city center and offers to those who appreciate such a warm friendly and attentive in a confined space (standing room only ...).

- Hosteria Dai Naneti Vicolo Broli, 2, For those who want to taste a bit 'of delicacies, drink a glass of wine and enjoy the atmosphere of the recent past by the Osteria Naneti in Treviso it is the right place. In the historic center, it looks like a shop of yesteryear where you can find everything: meats, cheeses and more. Entering discover, however, that you can gustarti delicious cicchetti, a sandwich expressed ...

- Carbone Via delle Medaglied'Oro 5 Piazzetta Caduti nei Lager 1943-45 +39 0422 348867 Small restaurant and a little 'Spartan to Treviso. It is close to a sports club, in a secluded corner so it may not be easy to locate. However as you enter you are greeted warmly and advised very well by the owner and that 'very helpful. The service is fast and professional, there is always someone who goes around the tables to check.

- Ristorantino L'Invito Viale Gian Giacomo Felissent, 52, +39 0422928087 Functional environment that creates the right atmosphere, excellent quality and freshness of the fish, excellent prosecco.

Venice day 1

At least two days should be spent in Venice.

St. Mark Square

Piazza San Marco

We start early in the morning from Piazza San Marco, the most beautiful drawing room in Europe, according to Napoleon, to avoid the midday crowds around St. Mark's Basilica and the Doge's Palace. Generations of artists and artisans have given it the appearance we now know, through ten centuries of uninterrupted labour; so that today the square in its entirety strikes us as a single complex work, a masterpiece of Italian taste and imagination.

Saint Mark's Basilica

San Marco Cathedral

In front of us is the Basilica di San Marco, founded in 828 and embellished uninterruptedly until the end of the 16th century. Greek and medieval, Byzantine and Tuscan, Lombard and Venetian art have contributed to its decoration, in every possible medium of expression, from mosaics to the work of goldsmiths, from sculpture to painting.

Opening hours:

Basilica: 9.45 a.m. - 5.00 p.m. - *Sunday and holidays:* 2.00 p.m. - 4.00 p.m. (entrance free)
St. Mark's Museum: 9.45 a.m. - 4.45 p.m. (entrance: 5 €)
Pala d'oro: 9.45 a.m. - 4.00 p.m. - *Sunday and holidays:* 2.00 p.m. - 4.00 p.m. (entrance: 2 €)

Treasury: 9.45 a.m. - 4.00 p.m. - *Sunday and holidays:* 2.00 p.m. - 4.00 p.m.(entrance: 3 €)

St Mark's Basilica

The Basilica is a wonderful example of Byzantine Venetian architecture. It was at one time the Doge's chapel but it was also the mausoleum for Saint Mark, the patron saint, whose life is narrated in the golden mosaics on the walls.

With five cupolas, it was built (10th century) to house the body of the St Mark the Evangelist.

The facade features five portals decorated in splendid marbles and mosaics, and with a terrace dividing it into two halves.

Saint Mark's horses

Four Horses

On the terrace stand Four Horses of gilded copper (copies – the originals are now preserved inside) that were sent from Constantinople to Doge Enrico Dandolo in 1204.

Splendid mosaics in the atrium relate the stories of the Bible.

The imposing interior in the form of a Greek cross contains a wealth of paintings and sculptures.

Saint Mark's Basilica interior

St Mark's interior

Of particular interest are mosaics of Venetian-Byzantine origin, some of them reconstructed from drawings by Titian, Tintoretto and Veronese.

The Bell Tower adjacent to the basilica was once a lighthouse for ships. At the foot of the tower is a 16th century loggia by J. Sansovino.

Doge's Palace

Doge's Palace

To the right of the Basilica, we go through the Porta delta Carta and into the Doge's Palace, built in the florid Gothic style typical of Venice (1303-1442). The Renaissance courtyard was designed by Antonio Rizzo (1483), who also left the two masterpieces of Venetian sculpture there, the statues of Adam and Eve (1464), now in the Doge's Apartments.

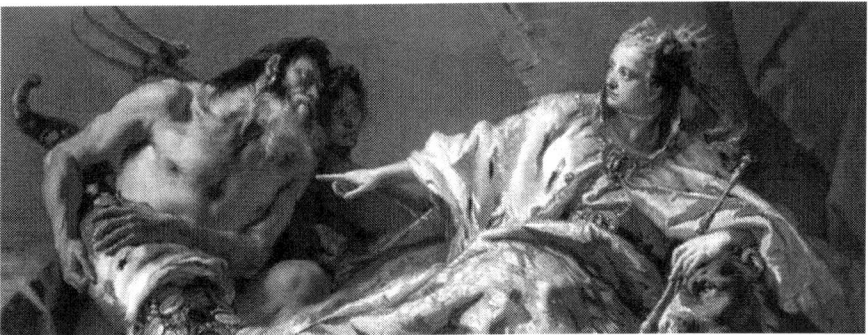

Tiepolo: *Neptune Offering Gifts to Venice*

Going up the Scala dei Giganti, we enter the incredibly lavish interior of the palace. It features carved and gilded ceilings, stuccoes, fireplaces and carved doors. It is one of the most gorgeous public residences of all times. Venetian painters, from Carpaccio to Gentile Bellini, from Titian to Veronese, and to Bassano, have created fantastic allegories, in which the glory of Venice, both in fact and in legend, is the dominating theme. We will be astonished by the gigantic canvas of Paradise by Tintoretto, the largest in existence.

Marvelous paintings hang on the walls, including the sublime Piety by Giovanni Bellini and three rare works by Hieronymus Bosch: Paradise, Hell and the Martyrdom of St. Juliana.

Opening hours of the Doge's Palace

from April 1st to October 31st
8.30 am – 7 pm (last admission 6 pm)

from November 1st to March 31st
8.30 am – 5.30 pm (last admission 4.30 pm)

The Piazzetta

Lion of St. Mark column

Leaving the Palace, we go and stand on the side of the Piazzetta facing the Lagoon; on top of the two columns (12th century), are statues of St. Theodore and of the Lion of St. Mark. Before our eyes, we have the light-filled panorama of St. Mark's Dock, at one time crowded with the fleet of the Republic.

The view is dominated by the Island of San Giorgio Maggiore: then to the left is the Lido, and the Riva degli Schiavoni; to the right, the Giudecca and the Customs-House Point and nearby the Basilica della Salute.

Procuratie Vecchie

Procuratie Vecchie at right

Opposite the Ducal Palace, stands the Libreria Vecchia, seat of the National Marciana Library, designed by Sansovino. Also by Sansovino is the stupendous Loggetta (1540) along the base of the Campanile. Extending down the two longer sides of the square are the Procuratie (ancient offices of the Venetian State). Next to the Procuratie Vecchie (1532) is the Clock Tower (1496) with its famous clock-work figures of the Moors.

Fabbrica Nueva

Procuratie Nuove at Carnival

The last section of the square, opposite St. Mark's, is known as the Fabbrica Nueva, or the Napoleonic ring, since it was built at the orders of Napoleon. Under the arcade of this side, we enter the Correr Museum, an important collection relating to civil and maritime history, of Venetian costumes and mementos, and magnificent paintings, including the Pieta by Antonello da Messina, the Trasfigurazione by Giovanni Bellini, and the Courtesans by Carpaccio.

Basilica della Salute

basilica della Salute

Leaving the square and passing the Baroque church of San Moise, we reach Santa Maria del Giglio, then take the nearby ferry and cross the Grand Canal to the Customs-House Point where, a few steps away, we come to the basilica della Salute, an architectural masterpiece of Baldassare Longhena (1631-1687). Inside, there are magnificent paintings by Titian, Tintoretto, Luca Giordano.

Riva delle Zattere

Zattere at Gesuati

Passing over a small bridge we come to the fine Gothic Abbey of San Gregorio, closed at present. Following the little canal, we reach the spacious Riva delle Zattere, across from the Giudecca.

Passing beyond the Lombard Church of the Holy Spirit, and going along the quayside by the red walls and gardens, we reach the Church of the Gesuati, which contains one of Tiepolo's finest canvases (Madonna and S. Caterina).

Church of the Gesuati

Gian Battista Tiepolo

The order of the Gesuati was suppressed in 1868 and the church and monastery were handed over to the Dominicans. In 1724 the architect Giorgio Massari was commissioned to build the new church. The inside has no side naves but contains altar pieces by Piazzetta, Sebastiano Ricci and Gian Battista Tiepolo.

The latter was also commissioned with decorating the ceiling with illustrations of the history of the Dominicans. The Gesuati church was rebuilt in 1657 on the site of a former church of the Crucifix Order.

The façade was paid for by the Manins and built by Fattoretto featuring baroque architecture with a very plastic character.

Accademia

Accademia Gallery

From here, we take the narrow, tree-lined street next to the church to the former church of the Carita on the Grand Canal. Today, this Gothic church forms part of the Accademia Galleries, the most important collection of paintings in Venice, the entrance to which is next door.

The **Gallerie dell'Accademia** is a museum gallery of pre-19th-century art. It is housed in the Scuola della Carità on the south bank of the Grand Canal, within the sestiere of Dorsoduro. It was originally the gallery of the Accademia di Belle Arti di Venezia, the art academy of Venice, from which it became independent in 1879, and for which the Ponte dell'Accademia and the Accademia boat landing station for the *vaporetto* water bus are named. The two institutions remained in the same building until 2004, when the art school moved to the Ospedale degli Incurabili.

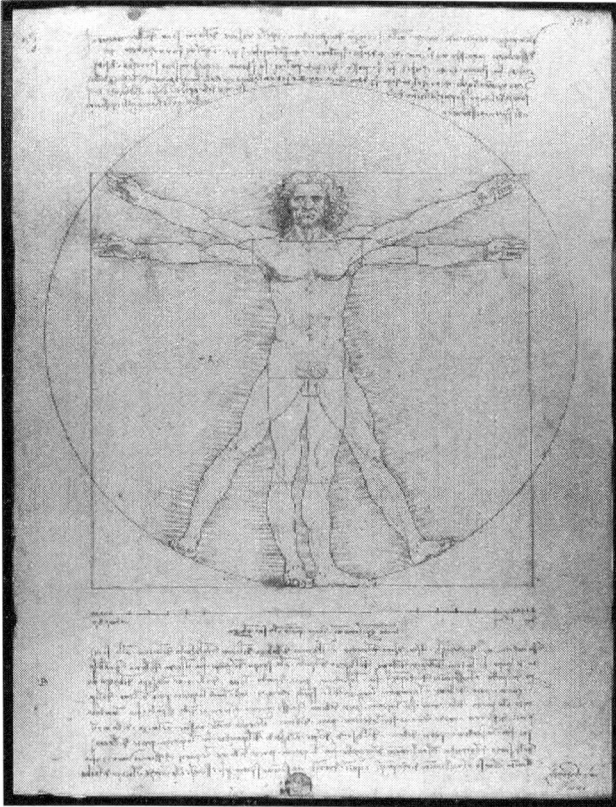

Leonardo da Vinci's Vitruvian man

Artists represented include: Lazzaro Bastiani, Gentile and Giovanni Bellini, Bernardo Bellotto, Pacino di Bonaguida, Canaletto, Carpaccio, Giulio Carpioni, Rosalba Carriera, Cima da Conegliano, Fetti, Pietro Gaspari, Michele Giambono, Luca Giordano, Francesco Guardi, Giorgione, Johann Liss, Charles Le Brun, Pietro Longhi, Lorenzo Lotto, Mantegna, Rocco Marconi, Michele Marieschi, Antonello da Messina, Piazzetta, Giambattista Pittoni, Preti, Tiepolo, Tintoretto, Titian, Veronese (Paolo Caliari), Vasari, Leonardo da Vinci (Drawing of Vitruvian Man), Alvise Vivarini, and Giuseppe Zais.

Ca' Rezzonico

Ca' Rezzonico

Leaving the Accademia, we go through the maze of narrow streets which take us to the 18th century church of S. Barnaba, and lead to Ca' Rezzonico, an imposing building designed by Longhena which houses paintings, marvelous furniture, costumes, ceramics, books, etc.

The palace was adapted to serve as the museum and opened to the public on April 25th 1936. The designers of the museum layout, Nino Barbantini and Giulio Lorenzetti, aimed to exploit the character of Ca' Rezzonico, arranging the works as if they were the palace's original furnishings. To achieve this result, numerous 18th century works that belonged to the other museums of Venice were moved to Ca' Rezzonico, together with paintings, furniture, and frescoes from other civic-owned buildings and many works purchased for the occasion.

The final effect was undeniably striking; the quality of the numerous works exhibited, together with the extraordinary quality of the architecture and the setting, made Ca' Rezzonico a veritable temple of the Venetian 18th century: an age of splendor, dissipation, and decadence, but undoubtedly one of the most lively and fertile seasons of modern art in Europe.

Scuola Grande di San Rocco (Confraternity)

Paintings in the sala superiore - Scuola Grande di San Rocco

Passing behind Palazzo Foscari, beyond the Rio Nuovo and the quaint Campo di S. Margherita, we come to the Church and School (1508-1530) of San Rocco. In the Great Hall of the School, Jacopo Tintoretto has left an incredible cycle of paintings (21 on the ceiling and 13 on the walls) which constitutes his masterpiece.

Located in the campo bearing the same name. In 1478, it was made into a charitable institution. The present building was started in 1489 and finished in the sixteenth century by the architect Giangiacomo dei Grigi. It is famous for displaying a series of paintings by Tintoretto that adorn the rooms. Next to the school there is the church, which is also dedicated to San Rocco. It was built in the sixteenth century and was renovated by Giovanni Scalfurotto in the eighteenth century. Built in the first half of the 16th C, the Guildhall of San Rocco is the home of an extraordinary cycle of canvases by J. Tintoretto, among which eight on the ground floor portray Scenes from the New Testament.

Tintoretto dedicated scenes taken from the Old Testament to the ceiling of the Upper Hall, while on the walls the cycle of paintings includes the great painter's self-portrait.

Church of the Frari (Santa Maria Gloriosa dei Frari)

Santa Maria Gloriosa dei Frari - interior

From here, we go to Santa Maria Gloriosa dei Frari, a solemn Gothic church whose interior is dominated by the luminous canvas of Our Lady of the Assumption by Titian (1518). Other paintings (Titian Bellini, etc.) and the numerous sculptures by great Venetian artists lend this church all the importance of a museum.

It was built in the fourteenth century by the Franciscans, who settled in Venice from about 1222. Rebuilt in the fifteenth century, it bears witness to the Venetian Republic with paintings by Titian and Bellini. It is an example of Gothic architecture from the middle of the fifteenth century, and has one of the highest bell towers in Venice, which was started in 1361.

Once known as Ca' Grande, erected between 1236 and 1338 through the efforts of the Conventual Franciscan Friars Minor, it was replaced by a grandiose Gothic Franciscan-style edifice in the 14th century, with a nave and two aisles and seven apsidal chapels.

The imposing 14th century brick bell tower is one of the highest in Venice. The Basilica is one of the most important sacred buildings owing to the wealth of artworks that it houses. The interior, in the Latin cross plan, features precious paintings such as one of the masterpieces of Titian's mature work, the Altarpiece of the Assumption (1516-1518), intended by the artist for the high altar.

Other works worthy of note are the Triptych of the Virgin and Saints by Giovanni Bellini (1488), located in the Pesaro Chapel of the Sacresty and considered to be one of the masterpieces of 15th century Venetian art, and the wooden statue of St John the Baptist, a superb work by Donatello.

Campo San Polo

Campo San Polo

A short walk brings us to the lively Campo San Polo, with its beautiful palaces, and if we continue parallel to the Grand Canal, which can be seen glinting at the ends of the various smaller canals, we reach the ancient little church of S. Giacomo a Rialto, with its large clock and its remarkable bell-tower, standing in the midst of the bustling market place.

Rialto Bridge

Rialto Bridge

Passing over the famous Rialto Bridge (1591), with its beautiful view of the Grand Canal, we reach Campo San Bartolomeo, and then turn right to the church of San Salvatore, the facade of which was designed by Sansovino and Scamozzi (inside, there is the Annunciation and Transfiguration by Titian).

Palazzo Contarini (called Del Bovolo)

Palazzo Contarini (called Del Bovolo)

Anybody can tell you the way to the 15th century Palazzo Contarini (called Del Bovolo), with its ingenious spiral staircase, and from there we can make our way to the elegant Campo Santo Stefano. with its austere 14th century church (paintings by B. Vivarini, Carpaccio, Piazzetta, Tintoretto).

Teatro della Fenice

Teatro della Fenice - interior

We can sit down in one of the cafes on the Campo to rest, before returning to Piazza San Marco by way of the Teatro della Fenice.

The Theater is one of the most famous and renowned landmarks in the history of Italian theatre as well as those in Europe. Especially in the 19th century, La Fenice became the site of many famous operatic premieres at which the works of several of the four major *bel canto* era composers—Rossini, Bellini, Donizetti, and Verdi were performed.

Its name reflects its role in permitting an opera company to "*rise from the ashes*" despite losing the use of three theaters to fire, the first in 1774 after the city's leading house was destroyed and rebuilt but not opened until 1792; the second fire came in 1836, but rebuilding was completed within a year. However, the third fire was the result of arson. It destroyed the house in 1996 leaving only the exterior walls, but it was rebuilt and re-opened in November 2004.

Day 2: Venice

Bridge of Sighs

The next day we set off from Piazza San Marco in the opposite direction. Passing by the Bridge of Sighs, with its romantic associations, and the adjoining Prison, we turn inland towards the church of San Zaccaria, a masterpiece of Venetian Renaissance architecture, designed by Coducci (1500). Inside, a famous Madonna by Giovanni Bellini, works by Tintoretto and in the gem-like chapel of S. Tarasio, polyptychs by Vivarini, Giovanni D'Alemagna and frescoes by the Florentine painter Andrea del Castagno may be seen.

From San Zaccaria, we go to the little church of S. Maria Formosa, in the square (campo) of the same name (featuring an important Triptych by B. Vivarini, and S. Barnaba by Palma il Vecchio). In the same square, too, is the Querini Stampalia Gallery, with an outstanding collection of Venetian paintings, especially from the 18th century, with the wonderful series of scenes of domestic and street life, painted by Pietro Longht. We come to Palazzo Prili, an extremely fine Venetian-Gothic building, and soon reach one of the sanctuaries of Venetian painting: the School of San Giorgio degli Schiavoni, containing the striking History of St. George, a series of pictures painted by Vittorio Carpaccio between 1501 and 1511.

S. Francesco della Vigna

S. Francesco della Vigna

We then come to the Palladian church of S. Francesco della Vigna (1572) with a delightful cloister (inside, a rare Madonna by Antonio da Negioponte, 1450, and paintings by Bellini, Vivarini, and Veronese; an important Lombard marble triptych in the Giustiniani Chapel), and then the vast Campo (square) which takes its name from the Church of San Giovanni e Paolo (1246-1430) the Pantheon of Venetian glories, with its severe aisled nave, paintings by Bellini and frescoes by Piazzetta as well as the magnificent tombs of illustrious Venetians. In the middle of the square, the vigorous statue of the famous Italian soldier of fortune, Bartolommeo Colleoni, executed by Andrea Verrocchio (1488) the teacher of Leonardo da Vinci. We suggest making a detour at this point to go and admire the flawless lines of S. Maria act Miracoli, designed by Pietro Lombardo (1489).

Returning to S. Giovanni e Paolo, we walk along the quaint Rio dei Mendicanti to the Fondamenta Nuove, and then along the side of the lagoon as far as the 18th century Church of the Jesuits, standing in a peaceful square of the same name. From here, we return to the Grand Canal to enjoy a veritable gem of Venetian Gothic architecture, the Ca' d'Oro (1421-1440) which contains the second most important picture gallery in Venice (the dramatic S. Sebastiano by Mantegna, a Venus by Titian, works by Vivarini, Carpaccio, Lippi, Ghirlandaio, Signorelli, etc.).

Campo dell'Abazia

Campo dell'Abazia

We now make for the solitary Gothic Church of the Misericordia and next to the School of the same name: this is one of the most picturesque spots in Venice, at the point where two canals are crossed by an attractive wooden bridge. We then carry on to the Church of the Madonna dell'Orto, where Tintoretto, who lived nearby and who is buried in the church, left another remarkable series of paintings. Returning to the Grand Canal, this time to stay, we come to the Palazzo Vendramini Calergi, where Richard Wagner died. We follow the Canal where, after crossing the Cannaregio, we discover the Church of San Geremia and the austere Palazzo Labia (16th century), which contains famous frescoes by Giovanni Battista Tiepolo.

Chiesa degli Scalzi

Church of the. Scalzi

Next to the railway station is the Church of the Scalzi with an 18th century facade. From here we take the ferry which will sail down the entire length of the Grand Canal and leave us at the Island of San Giorgio Maggiore, where there is a group of buildings dating from various periods, and dominated by the church designed by Andrea Palladio (1565-1980) which contains numerous paintings by Tintoretto and other artists.

We return to Piazza San Marco, where our Venetian tour comes to an end. It can be made more complete by taking four days for it, instead of two, following the same itineraries indicated above, but with detours and additions.

Cicchetti bars

Wine demijohns ready for the cicchetti bar

Venice, once a European superpower, but today, is just a small town of about 60,000 people. Yet it has more than 10 million visitors a year. There are no restaurants left in Venice that don't rely on tourists. *"But there are still the cicchetti bars."*

Venice has a wonderful tradition of *cicchetti* (pronounced chi-KET-tee) — the local appetizers that line the counters of little pubs all over town, but especially outside of the central tourist areas. You can visit a series of these characteristic hole-in-the-wall pubs, eating ugly-looking morsels on toothpicks, and washing it all down with little glasses of wine. An added advantage is that local characters surround you. And, in a town with canals and no cars, pub-crawling is safe and easy. Venetians call this pub crawl the *giro d'ombra.* Giro means stroll, and ombra — slang for a glass of wine — means shade.

Cicchetti bars have a social standup zone and a cozy gaggle of tables where you can generally sit down with your cicchetti or order from a simple menu. In some of the more popular places, the local crowds spill happily out into the street. Food usually costs the same price whether you stand or sit.

Chicchetti bars recommended by Timeout.com:

- Al Chioschetto Dorsoduro 1406A
- Al Vapore Via Fratelli Bandiera 8
- Alla Palanca Giudecca 448
- Angiò Castello 2142
- Aurora San Marco 48-50
- Dogado Lounge Cannaregio 3660A
- Il Caffè Dorsoduro 2963
- La Mascareta Castello 5183
- Orange Dorsoduro 3054A
- Ai Do Draghi Dorsoduro 3665
- Ai Postali Santa Croce 821
- Al Pesador San Polo 125-6
- Al Prosecco Santa Croce 1503
- Ardidos Cannaregio 2282
- Area Club Via Don Tosatto 9
- Bacaro Jazz San Marco 5546
- Bar ai Nomboli San Polo 2717C
- Bar all'Angolo San Marco 3464
- Café Blue Dorsoduro 3778

Where to eat in Venice

Restaurants in Venice:

- Dal Moro's - Fresh Pasta To Go Calle De La Casseleria, 5324 | Castello, +39 327 870 5014 Incredibly tasty and fresh pasta - all for a reasonable price too (around 7 euros). The staff is also very friendly and takes an interest in where you came from and what you were looking for in Venice. Something you don't expect! No surprise why this is rated so highly. Definitely worth a visit!

- Ristorante Alle Corone Castello, Campo della Fava 5527 +39 041 241 0253 The dining room is quite small, but that is, in no way a criticism. Go fairly early, and it is already busy, but you will not feel at any point cramped.
The service is absolutely outstanding – and the skill of the waiting staff was at points mesmerising (I'm not joking – watch them debone a Sea Bass!)
The food is excellent, and very fresh.

- Riviera Dorsoduro 1473 | Zattere - San Basilio, +39 041 522 7621 The staff, service, attention to detail and quality of food are exceptional. The need to provide a CC to confirm the booking is no issue; it is something I would expect of a restaurant in London and it does ensure that the booking is not a flippant one. The variety of the menu is great and the house red wines for starters and main course are lovely.

- Bacareto Da Lele Campo dei Tolentini 183 - Santa Croce, Little sandwiches, wine, a social event ordering, incredible value for the money! Two sandwiches and a glass of wine for less than €3!

- Osteria Alla Ciurma Calle Galeazza 406 - San Polo, +39 340 686 3561 This is a good place to try different small plate and you CANNOT beat the price here. Our glasses of wine were 1,50 and tasted amazing (we had the house red). IMPORTANT NOTE: get there early! They run out of items quickly and they do not make more once they do.

The Author

Enrico Massetti was born in Milano. Now he lives in Washington DC, USA, but he regularly visit his hometown, and enjoys going around all the places near his home town that can be reached by public transportation.

Enrico can be reached at enricomassetti@msn.com.

Photo Credits

Via Dante – Photo © Silvia Massetti
Castello Sforzesco – Photo © Silvia Massetti
Loggia dei Mercanti, via Mercanti – Photo © Silvia Massetti
The roof of the Duomo – Photo © Silvia Massetti
The Duomo from La Rinascente Cafe – Photo © Silvia Massetti
Galleria Vittorio Emanuele II – Photo © Silvia Massetti
Castello Sforzesco - Milan – Photo © Silvia Massetti
Brera – Photo © Silvia Massetti
Piazza Scala with the theater – Photo © Silvia Massetti
Via della Spiga – Photo © Silvia Massetti
Milan, villa Reale – Photo © Silvia Massetti
Bergamo Alta - Piazza Vecchia - Photo Public domain
A portico in the Old Town - Photo © Gabriele Motta
Basilica Facade - Photo Public domain
Panoramic view with Basilica di S. Maria Maggiore - Photo ©
Wooden Choir inlays - Photo © Sergio
Cappella Colleoni - Photo Public domain
Rocca di Bergamo - Photo © Giorces
Porta San Giacomo - Photo Public domain
Venetian Gates - Photo Public domain
Iseo Lake – Photo © RossiMarko81
Wine in Franciacorta – Photo © Piperita Patty
Franciacorta – Photo © Stefano Bonalumi
Tench – Photo © djordi
Old and New Cathedral
Piazza della Loggia – Photo © Antonino Faulisi
Mantova palazzo Ducale – Photo © telegraph.co.uk
Mantova at night – Photo © jimforest
Mantova, Palazzo Ducale – Photo © andrea castelli
Mantegna's fresco, the Gonzaga's court
Mantova Palazzo Te – Photo © Regione Lombardia
Palazzo Ducale – Photo © stijn
Mantova-camera-degli-sposi – Photo © B. Balestrini
San Giorgio Castle – Photo © Sebastia' Giralt
Tower of the Cage – Photo © Karsten B
Renaissance Porticos – Photo © Giovanna Marchese Occipinti
Palazzo della Ragione – Photo © Maurizio Codogno
Restaurants in Piazza Erbe – Photo © jimforest
Verona – Photo © www.telegraph.co.uk
Palazzo della Gran Guardia - Photo public domain
Museum of Gems and Jewelry - Photo Museum of Gems and Jewelry
Juliet's balcony - Photo Public domain
Villa Capra "La Rotonda" – Photo © Giav
Palazzo Thiene – Photo © machilin
Basilica Palladiana and Torre Bissara – Photo © sftrajan

Index

.

75554922R00073

Made in the USA
San Bernardino, CA
01 May 2018